PUBLIC POLICY IN INDIA

C-9: FOR B.A. 4TH SEMESTER STUDENTS OF BODOLAND UNIVERSITY ALSO
FOR GAUHATI UNIVERSITY

RITURAJ BASUMATARY

Made with ♥ on the Notion Press Platform
www.notionpress.com

Contents

CHAPTER ONE

Public Policy

Public Policy

Introduction

Public Policy is like a strategic framework which the government within a state uses to fulfill its functions. And in this regard, Public Policies become very significant as it holds the power to change and reshape the lives of the public in their given political system. The presence of Public Policy can be seen in every socio-economic aspects of public. States are enacting policies to bring economic development and promote social justice and empowerment of all sections of the society. A better understanding of Public Policy is very crucial for understanding the relationship between the state and its people.

In other words, Public Policy refers to the policy or plan of what to do and that is formulated and implemented for the benefit of the public. It relates to the plan of action to be pursued by the government.

Definitions of Public Policy

According to David Easton, "Public Policy is the authoritative allocation of values for the whole society."

Thomas Dye defines Public Policy as "whatever governments chooses to do or not to do."

Characteristics of Public Policy

1. Public Policy is goal oriented:- Public Policy is purposive. It is designed to achieve objectives based on societal and economic demands.

1. Public Policy is a course of action:- Public Policy is not just a decision rather it is a course of action which is designed and implemented based on a combination of decisions.

3. Public Policy is outcome of a strategic and ethical process:- Public Policy is designed and implemented to meet societal and economic requirements.

4. Public Policy is highly dynamic:- Public Policy is dynamic and changes with the changing issues in the environment.

5. Public Policy is a complex process:- There are social, economic relevance, national integrity and security, financial constraints, budget, infrastructure availability, validity of the information and data and so on which makes the Public Policy highly complex in nature.

6. Public Policy includes different components:- Public Policy is made of various structures, environment system and feedback mechanism. It comprises of environment which provides demands and support to the system.

7. Public Policy is based on guidelines:- Public Policy lays down the major policy guidelines. Based on that, policy is implemented. Policy guidelines inform about the principles of policy making and functioning of policy.

8. Public Policy is directed towards future:-Public Policy is based on objectives of public interest. Policy makes the future of a nation. More sound and holistic policies will be better for the nation.

Nature of Public Policy

Public Policy is in fact a skill because these tasks regularly some information about the social sciences and in this case, the stress is on the 'public policy' which is also known as 'government policy' and selected by a government as a direction for action. From the perspective of public policies, actions of government could be put broadly into two groups and they are:

1. Definite or Specific policies.
2. General, vague and inconsistent policies.

The public policy can be a positive or negative one, in its positive form, it can contain some system of evident government activity to treat a specific problem. Whereas, in the negative form, it might contain a decision by a public servant not to take action on some sort of matter on which the government action is required. These policies sometimes will have legally coercive so that people can adopt it legally for instance all the people will pay the taxes in order to stay away from the fines. These public policies makes public organizations different from private organizations.

Scope of Public Policy

The scope of Public Policy may be highlighted on the following broad areas:

1. Promotion of Social Welfare:- Policies pertaining to social welfare cover the problems pertaining to food, housing, health, education, social security, social welfare, employment etc.
2. Economic betterment:- Policies relating to economic affairs deal with activities of various sectors of the economy such as industry, agriculture, foreign trade and commerce, foreign exchange etc. for ensuring a prosperous and stable economy. It launches various schemes to train and educate the common people in different trades, occupations and skills.
3. Political advancement:- For the success of any political system, awareness on the part of the common people is essentialThis is more so about a democratic system.
4. Administrative efficiency:- Public Policies help to promote administrative efficiencydirectly as well as indirectly. This means that there may be policies, which are specifically formulated to and aim at enhancing efficiency of the administration.
5. Management of financial affairs:- The scope of Public Policy also covers the entire financial management of the government like circulation of money, foreign exchange and so on.
6. Environmental Protection:- Public Policies are also aimed at creating a healthy and clean environment, i.e. our sorroundings like maintainance of eco-balance, afforestation, soil conservation and so on.
7. Foreign affairs:- Public policies are also framed to promote and maintain international relations. Thus, maintenance of international peace, harmony and cooperation are the important areas covered under the scope of public policies.
8. Defense:- A state has also to frame policies in the field of defense as well. These policies includes both maintenance of internal order and defending its external boundaries.

9. The acid test of a country's development and progress is that how efficient it has developed its infrastructure. All the countries that are considered as developed in modern times have a well-developed infrastructure.

Stages/Subject-Matter of Public Policy

1. Formulating Public Policies

Governments, organisations and groups of people set and adopt procedural guidelines towards the achievement of their set goals and objectives. Policies are generally initiated to influence various environments, thereby addressing adverse effects that arise in those environments.

Public-Policy formulation involves the processes of studying and assessing issues that emerge as a potential threat and the impact they may have on the public. The public-policy formulation process intends to limit the identified consequences of a problem for the subject environments or invoke better performance of undertakings in the public sector.

Well-formulated policies are rational, specific in their statements and applicable to specific extents only. Such policies are not ambiguous and are effective in achieving the intended objectives. The process of public-policy formulation is intricate.

Creating a policy in order to oversee all stakeholders and pressure groups is a dangerous mistake. The civil society working together with the government is one way of ensuing democracy and collective representation. In the end, this enhances the effectiveness of the policy-formulation process.

For an effective policy-formulation process, it is crucial that staff is highly knowledgeable of and conversant with, institutional processes. Institutional processes encompass the determination of policy subject matter, implementation plans and designing and scrutinising the assessment and revision of public policies.

Thorough analysis based on the identified problems in public-policy formulation enhances the realisation of well-formulated policies; thus, mitigating the risks of unintended consequences emerging. Plans made for dealing with organisational setbacks in policy management play a significant part in raising the policy-formulation capability.

The process of creating public policy involves decision-making processes; it centres on making amendments during the implementation of public policies. This implies that the formulation and implementation of public policies works mutually, but not as two separate entities.

2. Implementing Public Policies

Policy implementation follows the process of policy formulation. Mazmanian and Sabatier describe policy implementation to include exercising particular policy decisions in a manner directed by the prescriptions of an administrator, law or court guidance. There are two main approaches to policy implementation: bottom–up and top-down.

The top-down approach is bureaucratic. Sabatier notes that it starts through a "policy decision and focuses on the extent to which its objectives are attained over time and why".

The establishment of the capacity of the implementation process to be consistent with causal theory, coupled with policy objectives, aims and goals is essential for a successful top-down process of policy implementation. The top-down approach to policy implementation is unidirectional. The process does not provide room for information flow through feedback channels.

The success of the top-down process of public-policy implementation is a function of the capacity of the legal frameworks and the enforcing agencies to force or compel groups of people targeted by the policy to abide by the policy guidelines. In the implementation of any policy, one determinant of success is how skilled the people charged with the implementation are.

Success in implementing a policy using the top-down approach is also dependent on socio-economic factors. The socio-economic factors have a role to play in policy implementation, as they constitute one of the measures used to assess the success of implementation.

The top-down approach requires political willingness as well as political support. May and Wintner maintain that the approach demands that the eventual success of the policy implemented should be measured by how well it is able to solve the problems that it was initially meant to offer solutions to.

The process divides the public-policy implementation process into two main segments. The first segment, the 'top', takes the role of the development of the policy. The 'bottom' constitutes the public-policy implementation agents. This segmentation ensures the flow of voice of command from the uppermost level to the lowest level in a single direction so that bureaucracy is enhanced during the implementation process.

A major challenge of using the top-down approach in the implementation of public policies is encountered when all issues affecting groups targeted by a given policy must be fully addressed in the implementation of that policy. As a result, researchers supporting the top-down approach, such as de Leon and de Leon and researchers opposed to it, such as Howlett, Ramesh and Perl fail to agree on an appropriate process for public-policy implementation.

Leon and de Leon state that bureaucrats constitute important agents for public policy implementation, although they are ignored by those who are charged with the role of implementing the top-down approach in public policy. The main argument here is that abiding by policy guidelines should not be a choice. Rather, it is mandatory.

As opposed to the top-down approach to policy-implementation process, the bottom-up approach integrates the groups of people targeted by a public policy into the implementation process. Sabatier notes that this step is initiated by "identifying the network of actors involved in service delivery in one or more local areas and asking them about their goals, strategies, activities and contacts".

The acquired contacts are then utilised in the development of myriads of networks with an objective of increasing the number of local, national and regional actors who would play the roles of financing, planning and executing the policy. In the bottom-up approach, 'top' as well as 'bottom' actors in the process of creating public policies collaborate and exchange information about policy formulation and implementation via a dynamic process.

The bottom-up approach maintains that the phases of policy implementation and formulation are inseparable. According to Pastine and Pastine, the approach views politicians and administrators as playing critical roles in the successful process of policy formulation followed by its implementation. Policy-making experts and politicians form the top level of the policy-making process.

The people whose problems a public policy seeks to solve form the bottom level. The need for a public policy emerges from the bottom. The response to these needs, however, is a responsibility of those at the 'top'. Sabatier criticises this direction of information flow in policy-making in the context of the bottom-up approach claiming that it is unidirectional because policy-making initiates from the 'bottom' and moves towards the 'top'.

The successful implementation of public policies requires the integration of the person affected by the policy in the planning, formulation and implementation phases of the policy.

Considering that the top-down public-policy implementation process is unidirectional and Sabatier argues that bottom-up approach is also unidirectional, hypothetically, perhaps the best approach to public-policy implementation is the one that encourages constant interaction between the 'top' and the 'bottom' actors in formulating and implementing public policy via forward and backward information-flow loops.

Such an approach can aid in capturing various intricacies that impede successful policy implementation. Efforts to ensure the identification of pitfalls to successful policy implementation highlight the need to evaluate public policy at the formulation and the implementation phases.

3. Evaluating Public Policies

The evaluation process encompasses an integral aspect of the process of making public policies. It aids in the identification and reflection on the unanticipated and anticipated outcomes of a policy. Evaluation is the process of measuring the efficacy, utility, advantages, disadvantages and the necessity of a particular process or physical installation.

The main objective of policy evaluation is to inform policy developers of the progress of policy implementation and to what extent the formulated policies under implementation are providing the anticipated outcomes.

When public-policy evaluators discover that policies being formulated or implemented have deficiencies that would cause those policies to fail to achieve the desired outcomes, evaluation becomes the tool for alerting policy-makers about the need to consider alternative policies.

It also helps in the correction of erroneous aspects of a policy during the process of implementation. Where the policy-implementation process yields the anticipated outcomes, evaluation is also crucial because it forms the justification for the legitimacy of public policy.

The evaluation process constitutes an important part of the learning process around policy-making. Evaluation is applied in the policy-making process as a scientific activity and a positivist exercise. It serves the functions of determining the quality, effectiveness, policy effects, capacity to achieve desired goals and the rationale for costs incurred in the formulation and implementation of public policies. In this context, evaluation does not form a discrete activity in the making of public policies. Rather, it is integrated into all processes of making public policy, including policy formulation and implementation.

4. Analysis

In the description section, policy evaluation was treated as a discrete activity, separate from the formulation and implementation of public policies. In this section, it is presented as an integral part of the implementation and formulation phases of public policies.

Types of Public Policy

1. Distributive Policy: These policies involve the allocation of resources to a certain population. In this type, costs are borne by the general population and the benefits are concentrated on a specific population. To put it to perspective, the resources used in these policies are the taxes collected from every citizen of the country and it is used to provide beneficial programs and projects to a specific group or individuals.

2. Regulatory Policy: These policies are intended to limit the activities of specific individuals and groups to protect the people. In this category, the costs are concentrated on a specific population for the benefit of the more general population. These policies are often aimed at safeguarding our welfare and allowing us to experience a better quality of life.

3. Redistributive Policy: These policies entail taking resources from one group while allocating these taken resources to benefit another group. Here, the costs are concentrated on a specific group and its benefits are also concentrated on another group. Though, often, we see this policy as a way of the government to redistribute wealth and promote equality in society. It's not always the case.

4. Substantive Policy: These policies are tangible actions taken by the government towards the people's concerns. It directly affects the welfare of its beneficiaries and the population that were identified to carry the cost in achieving the policy goals.

5. Procedural Policies: These policies are actions taken by the government towards their structures and processes. It deals with the adjustments and developments on the methods that the government uses to perform their task. It affects the way the government accomplishes their duties – which includes the creation of public policies.

Models of Public Policy Making

1. Institutional Model

Focuses on the traditional organization of government. Describes the duties and arrangements of bureaus and departments. Considers constitutional provisions, administrative and common law, and judicial decisions. It focuses on formal arrangements such as federalism executive reorganizations, presidential commission, etc. Traditionally political science has studied government institutions--Congress, presidency, courts, political parties, etc.--that authoritatively determine, implement, and enforce public policy. Strictly speaking, a policy is not a public policy until it is adopted, implemented and enforced by some governmental institution.

Government lends legitimacy to policies, they are then legal; Government extends policies universally to cover all people in society; Government monopolizes the power to coerce obedience to policy or to sanction violators.

Traditional studies using the institutional approach focused on institutional structures, organization, duties and function, without investigating their impact on public policy.

2. Elite-Mass Model

A policy-making elite acts in an environment characterized by apathy and information distortion and governs a largely passive mass. Policy flows downward from the elite to the mass. Society is divided into those who have power and those who do not. Elites share values that differentiate them from the mass. The prevailing public policies reflect elite values, which generally preserve the status quo. Elites have hither income, more education and higher status than the mass. Public policy may be viewed as the values and preferences of a governing elite. The elites shape mass opinion more than vice versa. Public officials and administrators merely carry out policies decided on by the elite, which flows 'down' to the mass. It assumes that

1) society is divided into the powerful few and the powerless many; only the few allocate values (the mass do not decide public policy).

2) The few are not typical of the mass; elites are drawn disproportionately from the upper strata.

3) There must be slow and continuous movement of non-elites into elite positions, but only after they accept elite values in order to maintain stability and avoid revolution.

4) All elites agree on basic social system and preservation values i.e. private property, limited government and individual liberty.

5) Changes in public policy will be incremental rather than revolutionary, reflecting changes in elite values (not mass demands).

6) Active elites are subject to little influence from apathetic masses.

Implications are that the responsibility for the state of things rests with the elites, including the welfare of the mass. The mass is apathetic and ill-informed; mass sentiments are manipulated by the elite; the mass has only an indirect influence on decisions and policy. As communication flows only downward, democratic popular elections are symbolic in that they tie the mass to the system through a political party and occasional voting. Policies may change incrementally but the elites are conservative and won't change the basic system. Only policy alternatives that fall within the range of elite value consensus will be given serious consideration. Competition centers around a narrow range of issues and elites agree more than they disagree; there is always agreement on constitutional government, democratic procedures, majority rule, freedom of speech and of the press, freedom to form political parties and run for office, equality of opportunity, private property, individual initiative and reward and the legitimacy of free enterprise and capitalism. The masses cannot be relied on to support these values consistently, thus the elite must support them.

3. Group Model

Public policy results from a system of forces and pressures acting on and reacting to one another. Usually focuses on the legislature, but the executive is also pressured by interest groups. Agencies may be captured by the groups they are meant to regulate and administrators become increasingly unable to distinguish between policies that will benefit the general public and policies that will benefit the groups being regulated. Interaction among groups is the central fact of politics. Individuals with common interests band together to press their demands (formal or informally) on government. Individuals are important in politics only when they act as part of or on behalf of group interests. The group is the bridge between the individual and the government.

The task of the political system is to

1) establish the rules of the game

2) arrange compromises and balance interests

3) enact compromises in public policy

4) enforce these compromises

It is also called equilibrium theory as in physics. Influence is determined by numbers, wealth and organizational strength, leadership, access to decision makers and internal cohesion. Policy makers respond to group pressure by bargaining, negotiating and compromising among competing demands. Executives, legislators and agency heads all put together coalitions from their consistencies to push programs through. Political parties are coalitions of groups. The Democrats have traditionally been central city, labor, ethnics/immigrants, the poor, Catholics, liberals, intellectuals, blacks and Southern blue collar workers. Republicans have been wealthy, rural, small town, whites, suburbanites, white collar workers, conservatives and middle class.

The entire system assumes:

1) a 'latent' group supports the rules of the game

2) there is overlapping group membership which keeps groups from moving too far out of the political mainstream

3) there are checks and balances on groups competition

4. Systems Model

Relies on information theory concepts such as input, output and feedback. Sees the policy process as cyclical. Asks "what are the significant variables and patterns in the public policy-making system?" What goes on within the 'black box' of conversion of demands into public policy? What are the inputs and outputs? Public policy is viewed as the response of the political system to forces brought to bear on it from the outside environment. The environment surrounds the political system. In this model "environment" means physical: natural resources, climate, topography; demographic: population size, age and distribution and location; political: ideology, culture, social structure, economy and technology. Forces enter the political system from the environment either as demands or as support. Demands are brought to it by persons or groups in response to real or perceived environmental conditions for government action. Support is given wherever citizens obey laws, vote, pay taxes, etc. and conform to public policies.

The political system is a group of interrelated structures and processes that can authoritative allocate resources for a society. The actors are the legislature, the executive, the administrative agencies, the courts, interest groups, political parties and citizens.

Outputs are decisions and actions and public policy. The political system is an identifiable system of institutions and processes that transform inputs into outputs for the whole society. The elements with the system are interrelated and it can respond to forces in the environment and it seeks to preserve itself in balance with the environment. The system preserves itself by producing reasonably satisfactory outputs (compromises are arranged, enacted and enforced). It relies on deep rooted support for the system itself and its use or threat of use of force.

Macro level policies are those that concern the whole system and are influenced by official and unofficial groups (media, etc.). It may center on the proper role of Congress or the President or the relationships of government and business or citizens and businesses. Subsystem policies involve legislators, administrators and lobbyists and researchers who focus on particular problem areas; also called sub-governments, policy clusters, coalitions or iron triangles. E.G. civil aviation, harbors, agricultural subsidies, grazing lands, etc. Micro-level policies are efforts by individuals, companies or communities to secure some favorable legislation for themselves. Typically presented to a legislator as a request from the "home" district. The incentive to engage in micro-politics increases as the extent of government benefits, programs and regulations increases.

5. Streams and Windows Model

This model posits three streams which are always simultaneously ongoing. When the three streams converge, a policy window opens and a new policy may emerge. The problem stream focuses the public's and policy-makers' attention on a particular problem, defines the problem and calls for a new policy approach (or else the problem fades). Attention comes through monitoring data, the occurrence of focusing events and feedback on existing polices though oversight studies os program evaluation. Categorization of the problem is important in determining how the problem is approached and/or resolved: values, comparisons and categories.

The political stream is where the government agenda is formed: the list of issues or problems to be resolved by government. This occurs as the result of the interaction of major forces such as the national mood, organized interests and dynamics of public administration (jurisdictional disputes among agencies, the makeup of government personnel, etc.). The players are often quite visible as members of the administration, appointees and staff, Congress, medica, interest groups, those associated with elections, parties and campaigns and public opinion. A consensus is achieved among those groups and a bandwagon effect or title effect occurs as everyone wants to be in on the policy resolution and not excluded.

The policy stream is where alternatives are considered and decisions are made. Here the major focus in intellectual and personal; a list of alternatives is generated from which policy makers can select one. Policy entrepreneurs and other play a role, such as academics, researchers, consultants, career public administrators, Congressional staffers, OMB staff and interest groups. Trial balloons are sent up to gauge the political feasibility of various alternatives, either publicly or privately. They must be acceptable in terms of value constraints, technical constraints and budgetary constraints. Consensus is developed though rational argument and persuasion (not bargaining). Tilt occurs when a plausible solution begins to emerge.

When these three streams converge, a policy window may open because of a shift in public opinion, a change in Congress or a change in administration or when a pressing problem emerges. Any one stream may change on its own, but all three must converge for a policy decision to emerge.

Public Policy Process in India

Introduction

Policy-making is a continuing process. It does not come to an end once a policy is approved or adopted. As Anderson observes: "Policy is being made as it is being administered and administered as it is being made." Yet, each stage or phase of the policy process -formulation, implementation, evaluation-differs from the other. The policy process consists of stages of policy activity such as formulation, implementation and evaluation. Birkland observes that 'policy process' is a "system that translates policy ideas into formulation, implementation, evaluation actual policies that are implemented and have positive effects." For example, the main characteristics of the Eastonian (systems) model is that of viewing policy process in terms of received inputs (demand, support), in the form of flows from the environment, mediated through input channels (interest groups, media); demands within the political system (with inputs) and their conversion into policy outputs.

Stages in the Policy Process

Thomas Dye (2004) sets out the following stages in his analysis of the policy process:

1) Problem Identification: The identification of policy problems through demands for government action.

2) Agenda Setting: Focusing the attention of the mass media and public officials on specific public problems as a prelude to decision making.

3) Policy Formulation: The development of policy proposals by interest groups, officers of the chief executive's office, committees of the legislature, think tanks, etc.

4) Policy Legitimation: The selection and enactment of policies through political actions by the executive, the legislature and the courts.

5) Policy Implementation: The implementation of policies through organised bureaucracies, public expenditures and the activities of executive agencies.

6) Policy Evaluation: The evaluation of policies by government agencies themselves, outside consultants, the press and the public. Hogwood and Gunn have identified nine important stages in the policy process: deciding to decide (agenda setting), deciding how to decide (issue filtration), issue definition, forecasting, setting objectives and priorities, options analysis, policy implementation, monitoring and control, evaluation and review and policy maintenance, succession and termination. The policy cycle of May and Wildavsky (1978) includes agenda-setting,

issue analysis, implementation, evaluation and termination. Similarly, James Anderson has also dealt with description of the policy process. His model of the policy process has five stages: (i) problem identification and agenda formulation (ii) formulation (iii) adoption (iv) implementation and (v) evaluation.

There are basic linkages in a policy framework for the systematic analysis of information and its use in a policy-related context. The basis to the framework is information for policy analysis, which is derived from system or programme performance in terms of interaction among inputs, which indicate needs and demands processes concerning the provision of services for long-term care outputs in terms of the use of services and cost of care outcomes, which identify the end results of certain courses of action. For example, in the context of the National Health Policy (2017), the inputs (in terms of need and demands) comprise health, illness and the quality of life, expressed in physical, psychological, social and environmental terms. Needs are the conditions that call for action. They are among the most important predictors of utilisation and are mostly described in terms of diagnosis, functional limitation, perceived illness, symptoms or poor health status. On the other hand, demands are expressed as desires in relation to the services sought, whether they are needed or not. Other inputs include resources, such as manpower (doctors, nurses and para-medical staff) hospitals, primary health centres, medical equipment and facilities, medicine and performance standards. On the process linkage, it is concerned with the delivery of services to meet the needs and demands of clients and professionals. Services are described in such terms as their types, delivery, management and controls of cost and quality. Other services include supports such as legal aid, income support, consumer education and professional development. The outputs of service related programmes are described in terms of the use of those services, the costs and the quality of care. Finally, the outcomes are the responses to the services expressed in terms of the levels of well-being and health and client and professional satisfaction that are attained as a result. The foregoing analytical framework facilitates programme evaluation, which is expected to lead to rational policies and decisions about health services. In the next section, we will describe the various stages in policy process.

Identifying Underlying Problem

For an analytic approach, the first step is to identify whether and why there is a problem at all. Defining the problem involves moving from mundane descriptions to a more abstract, conceptual plane. Here, an attempt is be made to diagnose the form of market failure that is confronted. For example, an environmentalist who is investigating alternative pollution control measures for the Ganges will find that the water is being polluted by the dumping of industrial wastes and untreated sewage into the river. Having identified the context of the problem, the next step is to determine what objectives are to be achieved in tackling the issue. Too often, we lose sight of the basic objectives. Paying careful attention to the objectives is, therefore, important. For example, the provision of the services of doctors is merely a means to the end of improving people's health.

Determining Policy Alternatives

The next step is to determine alternative courses of action. Government intervention can take any form. It is important to determine which kind of intervention is most positive in a given situation. In the case of pollution of the Ganges, consider the following possibilities: i) Abutters in some catchments or adjoining areas of the river might be put under an obligation by the government to clean water. The government would then have the right to sue a polluter. ii) The government may require the industrialists concerned and urban dwellers concerned to stop dumping waste and untreated sewage into the river. It may otherwise impose restrictions on them on the quantity of dumping. The government may permit polluters to purchase rights to discharge a certain amount of pollutants. Polluters may be required to pay effluent charges and to install pollution control devices. iii) The state government or the local authority itself can directly undertake the work of cleaning and removing the pollutants that others dump. These are some of the alternatives for pollution control. As difficulties are identified and additional information becomes available, refinement of alternative courses of action will continue throughout the analysis. Determining alternatives for policy choice generally requires expertise or special knowledge in the relevant areas.

Forecasting and Evaluating Alternatives

Having identified the underlying problem and having determined the alternatives for policy choice, the policy analyst evaluates the consequences of each of the alternatives. For this, he will turn to a relevant model for forecasting consequences. In the case of the pollution control problem, the models needed would be far more complex. It is necessary here to predict all the effects of the proposed policies, not just the economic effects desired by the decision-maker. If the consequences of an alternative course of action are uncertain and especially if the possible outcomes differ widely from one another, the analyst may wish to develop a decision tree and evaluate the probability of each outcome. Very often it is difficult to have a rational policy choice unless the relative merits of alternative options are analysed systematically. The costs involved in regulation and administration needs to be evaluated. Evaluation of the outcomes is of great importance as it reminds us to look carefully at the cost-benefit analysis of a particular policy choice.

Policy Selection

The next step in policy analysis relates to making the preferred choice (course of action). The situation may be so simple for the policy-maker that he can simply look at the consequences predicted for each alternative and select the one that is best. In contrast, it may be so complex that the policy analyst will have to set out the order of preferences among the various possible outcomes, that is, in terms of how different sets of stakeholders might respond to the possible choices and their outcomes. It has been observed that countless policy studies have led nowhere. Sometimes the fault is attributed to the public decision-makers who do not take advantage of readily accessible data. Too often, it is the analysts themselves who have to share a major portion of the blame when things go wrong. But, by enhancing the capability of the analyst to forecast the consequences of the alternative courses of actions and providing a framework for evaluating those consequences, the techniques of policy analysis lead to better decisions and policies.

Implementation (Policy Action)

In the final analysis, the success of public administration can be measured only in relation to the implementation of policies. Policy implementation is of critical importance to the success of government. However good the political system, however noble the goals, however sound the organisational system, no policies can succeed if the implementation is poor. In its most general form, implementation is a phase between a policy statement and operation. It seeks to determine whether an organisation is able to carry out and achieve the stated objectives of its policies. The exercise involves developing and pursuing a strategy of organisation and management to ensure that the policy process is completed with the minimum of delays, cost overruns and problems. More specifically, the task of implementation is to form a bridge that allows the objectives of public policies to be achieved as outcomes of governmental activity. It involves the creation of a policy delivery system in which specific mechanisms are designed and pursued in the hope of reaching particular ends.

Constraints in Policy Implementation

Policies can become very difficult to implement if the implementers are not given sufficient autonomy and flexibility in carrying out their tasks. Political pressures in a democratic context constitute a major constraint. A third constraint is that the bureaucracy does not have the necessary professional skills needed for the implementation of the policies. Lack of resources such as personnel, financial and technical also becomes a hindrance in the implementation of public policy. Another problem in policy implementation might arise due to lack of response from the target groups. Sometimes, people do not evince adequate interest in the implementation of a programme;

because they may not be aware of the objectives and goals of a programme. Lack of people's participation often upsets implementation.

Policy Monitoring

Monitoring is essentially a subset of the implementation process. It is an activity which occurs in the course of implementing a policy or programme. It is in the process of monitoring that the implementer actually gets to begin seeing the results of policy. The objective of policy monitoring is to ensure through the policy implementation process that resource inputs are used as efficiently as possible to yield intended results. The standards which are used for both efficiency of resource utilisation and effectiveness of policy implementation are inherent in the policy-making process. The monitor has to be able to appraise resource use, technical activities and policy implementation results with an amount of detail which permits him to make changes or corrections when necessary. An effective monitoring of public policies aids in cost reduction, time saving and effective resource utilisation. The key issue in monitoring is to create an information system that enables policy makers and policy implementers to make timely decisions and policies. Therefore, it is important that monitoring and control processes should be given due importance and be designed properly. One of the serious problems in monitoring relates to poor design of the implementing system. Second, time is a constraint for policy monitoring. Too often, the implementing staff feels so pressed to achieve results that they take shortcuts and avoid monitoring and control. Third, a common constraint for the policy implementation manager is the shortage of corrective actions, which would be applied when the programme is found to be deviating in some respect from projected performance. Fourth, a pervasive obstacle to policy monitoring is ignorance about its role and methods. This is often due to lack of requisite skills on the part of the key functionaries.

Policy Outcomes

The next stage in the policy cycle is the policy outcomes. They are different from outputs. Policy outputs are the actual decisions of the implementers. The concept of outcomes lays stress on what actually happens to the target groups intended to be affected by the policy. If the intended changes on target groups do not occur, something is wrong. State housing schemes for the poor may be used to illustrate this point. Although one can find the fulfilment of targets, including the physical presence of houses, it was observed that in a majority of the instances the beneficiaries choice not to occupy them because they were not to their liking in terms of the size, ambience or quality of construction or some other deficiencies. The policy outputs were achieved, but not the outcomes.

Policy Evaluation

The final stage of the policy process in the sequential pattern of activities is the evaluation of policy. Evaluation is concerned with what happens, once a policy has been put into effect. It is an assessment of the overall effectiveness of a programme in meeting its objectives or assessment of the relative effectiveness of programmes in meeting the expected objectives. Evaluation performs several functions in policy analysis. In the first place, it provides reliable information about policy performance. It measures the impact of policies on society. It reveals the extent to which particular goals have been achieved (for example, increase in the life expectancy at birth). It also helps us to understand the degree to which policy issues have been resolved. Secondly, evaluation helps clarify the values that underline the selection of goals and objectives. Thirdly, evaluation may result in efforts to restructure policy problems. It may also contribute to the emergence of new goals and potential solutions. Evaluation during the implementation process of a policy might suggest its termination of the political together. In short, evaluation is primarily an effort to analyse policy outcomes in terms of the set objectives. It is, therefore, helpful in bringing out the utility of the policies under consideration.

Design of Evaluation

Evaluating a public programme involves the listing of the goals of the programme, measuring the degree to which these goals have been achieved and finally suggesting changes that might bring the performance of the organisation more in line with the intended purposes of the programme. Evaluation has a sensitive side of it. It may sometimes become a point of conflict or reinforce pre-existing conflicts. Negative evaluation of the performance of a public programme may result in its termination. The content of an evaluation, the goals that are contained in it and even the organisation performing the functions, all of them will affect the final assessment. Therefore, there is a need for a careful design of evaluation work by competent persons. This requires adequate information feedback, resources and political will.

Formulation of Public Policy

Constitutional Framework for Policy-Making

Policy-making in India is shaped within the framework of the constitutional system of which four features stand out most prominently: democratic and sovereign republic, parliamentary system, the federal character of the Constitution and a broad socio-economic philosophy - reflected especially in the preamble, the chapters on Fundamental Rights and the Directive Principles of the state policy.

Institutional Factors

In addition to these four constitutional factors there are other factors that govern policy-making in India.

Legislature

Parliament in India is the supreme public policy-making body. It reigns supreme because the council of ministers headed by the Prime Minister is dependent upon the support of a parliamentary majority to remain in force. It enacts laws which will bring the policies into effect. It also legitimises the policy decisions of the government. In reality, however, it does not reign supreme. It does not determine policies except in a formal sense. It influences public policies through general discussions and debates. Most of the legislation in India is prepared within the executive and introduced in the legislature by the minister concerned. The executive is assured of a legislative majority for the policy proposals it presents.

Executive

It is the constitutional task of the executive to decide the policies which are to be submitted to Parliament. The executive at the Union level in India consists of the President of India, the Council of Ministers and the machinery of government. The main bodies engaged in policy formulation in the executive are:

i) Cabinet:

The real executive is the Council of Ministers consisting of the Prime Minister, cabinet ministers, ministers of state and the deputy ministers. It is well-known that the Council itself hardly meets and all the policy functions are performed by the Cabinet.

ii) The Prime Minister:

Within the Council of Ministers in general and the cabinet in particular, the Prime Minister enjoys a special position in the realm of policy-making. The Prime Minister is expected to exercise control over the cabinet decision-making process.

iii) Secretariat-Department and Ministry: The secretariat is an administrative organisation to assist the government in the discharge of its executive and legislative responsibilities. It is a complex of departments and ministries whose administrative heads are known as secretaries and whose political heads are the ministers. The secretary acts as the chief adviser to the minister. He assists the minister(s) in the formulation of public policies. As policies can be framed only on the basis of availability and adequacy of data, the secretariat makes relevant information available to the minister, thus helping him to formulate policies.

Judiciary

The judiciary in India also plays a constructive role in shaping and influencing public policies in two ways: a) by its power of judicial review and b) judicial decisions. The Constitution empowers the Supreme Court and High Courts at the state levels to exercise a judicial review of legislation. Judicial review is the power of the courts to determine the constitutionality of actions of the legislature and the executive. They are not only specifying the government's limits with regard to certain actions, but also stating what it must do to promote public interest. Besides, the higher judiciary is also exercising its influence through its decisions in Public Interest Litigation cases.

Non-Governmental Institutions

Some non-governmental organisations such as political parties, pressure groups, media and citizenry are also informal participants in the policy process. Their views and influence are of critical value to the policy-making process.

Political Parties and Pressure Groups

The pressure exerted by pressure groups and political parties is an important factor in the making of policies. The political parties provide impetus to policies through their election manifestoes and by enlisting support at the time of elections. Pressure groups strive to influence the decisions of the government in manifold ways. Often, these groups are found to have conflicting values on a particular policy issue. Obviously, well-organised and active pressure groups have more influence than groups whose members are poorly organised and inarticulate.

The Individual Citizen and the Media

The people initiate the process of legislation and policy-making by voting for candidates with specific policy preferences. A democratic government is supposed to reflect the wishes of the people. Yet, in reality citizen's participation in policy-making is very negligible. Acting alone, the individual citizen is rarely a significant political force. The media can also influence public opinion in a situation. Media influence, however, depends upon the level of responsiveness from the government.

External Agencies Influencing Policy

External agencies and non-state actors are an important source in the initiation of new public policies or modification of pre-existing policies, especially in Third World countries like India. They include agencies such as the United Nations and its allied agencies (WHO, ILO, UNEP, UNDP, etc.), the World Bank, the International Monetary Fund, the Organisation for Economic Cooperation and Development (OECD) and other multilateral agencies is of critical importance in shaping policy outcomes.

Policy Implementation
Importance and Meaning

In the final analysis, the success of public administration for development can be measured only in relation to the implementation of policies. Implementation determines the extent to which an organisation is able to carry out and achieve the stated objectives. It involves developing and pursuing a strategy to ensure that the policy process is completed with the minimum of delays, costs and problems. Implementation involves the "creation of a policy delivery system in which specific mechanisms are designed and pursued in the hope of reaching particular ends". Thus, public policies in the form of statement of goals and objectives are put into action-programmes that aim to realise the ends stated in the policy. Putting policy into effect involves not the end of policy-making, but a continuation of policy-making by other means. At the minimum, implementation requires: 1) adequate personnel and the financial resources to implement the policy; 2) the administrative capability to achieve the desired policy goals; and 3) support from the legislative, executive and judicial wings of the government for the successful implementation of policy.

Implementers

Public Policies in India, as in other countries, are implemented by a complex system of administrative organisations and agencies. The main agency which implements government activities and public policies is the bureaucracy. This is an important institution which performs most of the day-to-day work of government. It is the bureaucracy which controls the personnel, money and other resources of the government and has legal authority for their deployment. Since so much power and control over implementation is held by the bureaucracy the legislature, the chief executive and judiciary set limits to its discretion and indirectly control its excesses, if any. Though discretion and delegation are inevitable in a complex policy apparatus specific strategies exist to exercise control over bureaucracy's operations if things go wrong. In the process the legislature and the judiciary tend to participate in policy implementation.

Conditions for Successful Implementation

Implementation is seen varying along a continuum ranging from most successful to failure. Successful implementation involves many operations and procedures as well as time and resources. Sabatier and Mazmanian (1979) identify five conditions for effective policy implementation.

These are:

1) The programme is based on sound assumptions relating changes in target group behaviour in consonance with the programme objectives.

2) Unambiguous policy directives and structures of the implementation process to enable target groups to maximise their performance.

3) The leaders of the implementation agencies possess substantial managerial and political skill and are committed to statutory goals.

4) The programme is actively supported by organised groups and by a few key legislators (or the chief executive) throughout the implementation process, with the judiciary being neutral or supportive.

5) The relative priority of statutory objectives is not significantly undermined over time by the emergence of conflicting public policies or by change in relevant socio-economic conditions.

Policy-making does not end once a decision is reached. The implementation of a decision is just as important as the policy itself. No policy formulator can assume that decisions will automatically be implemented as envisioned.

Policy implementation requires a wide variety of actions, including,

a) issuing policy directives that are clear and consistent;

b) creating organisational units and assigning personnel with the information and authority necessary to administer the policies;

c) coordinating personnel resources and expenditures to ensure benefit to target groups; and

d) evaluating implemental actions of the personnel.

None of these steps is easy. The implementation of policy thus involves not the end of policy-making, but a continuation of policy-making by other means.

Policy-Making Process in India

Policy-making is a vital function at all levels of government in India. For the conduct of government business, certain rules have been framed under Article 77(3) of the Constitution. The Rules of Business govern the procedure for decision-making and within the ambit of these rules, policy decisions are taken by the Council of Ministers, particularly by the cabinet. But nowhere in the rules does there seem to be any distinction drawn between those decisions which are concerned with policy and those that are not. Policy and administration are intimately related and are an integral part of executive government. Indeed, it may be said that some important decisions on policy are often taken informally. The Prime Minister or a particular colleague, if he is confident of being able to carry a particular policy through, may announce a decision, either in parliament or in public. However, this is not frequent, especially in a coalition government. The cabinet makes use of the committee system to facilitate decision making in specific areas. Depending upon the membership of any cabinet committee, its decision is either final on behalf of the government, or its decision may be placed before the full cabinet committee for ratification. A vast number of decisions are, of course, taken by individual ministers within the ambit of the rules for the business of the government and these are considered as authoritative decisions of the government. It often depends upon the personality and political image of a minister as to what matters he will decide, and what he will refer to the Prime Minister or to the cabinet. But the cabinet as a whole has to be persuaded of the rightness of such decisions. It is, therefore, observed that cabinet decisions are taken by the Prime Minister together with the minister concerned. Technically speaking, most of the decisions on various matters involving policy issues of less importance are taken by the administrative secretaries or committee of secretaries some of which service a cabinet committee. The secretary to government in the particular ministry, senior civil servants of the ministry, heads of government departments and other officials at levels below the departmental heads are vested, in specific matters, with delegated authority. For the conduct of government business, there are large volumes of departmental rules of procedure and of guidance in the making of decisions in each particular agency. Where a matter is seen to be of concern or interest to a ministry or department other than the one in which it is being considered, it is incumbent upon the former to consult the affected ministry or department at the appropriate levels. This is a somewhat sketchy account of the policy making process and decision-making procedures. In a complex system such as the Union government or that of a State government in India, a vast number of social, political, economic and administrative factors influence the choice of a policy. The election manifesto of the political party in power, interest groups, political parties, the administrative and judicial courts, the NITI Aayog, the Goods and Service Tax Council, a system of centre-state consultations, international agencies or other non-state actors and many other institutions have functions with a direct or indirect bearing on policy-making. Thus, within the constitutional ambit, these institutions or their decisions may exercise influence on government policy. The extent of influence may vary, depending upon a wide range of contextual factors. The policy-making process has, to a large extent, been regarded, by David Easton, as a 'black box' which converts demands into policies but whose structure is seen to be unknown and inaccessible to observation. Policy-making is "an extremely complex analytical and political process to which there is no beginning or end and the boundaries of which are most uncertain" (Lindblom, 1968). Somehow, a complex set of forces engage in 'policy-making', Public Policy and taken as a whole, produce effects, called policies. The Parliament is empowered by the Indian Constitution with the function of representing the people in making policy through the passing of laws. The legislative process is, therefore, a fundamental mechanism for expressing public policy. At the same time, legislation permits more specific policy-making by the executive branch of the government within the legislative and constitutional framework, and the review functions of the judiciary.

Conclusion

The use of the policy process can bring benefits to the analysis of public policy. Perhaps more attention could have been paid to implementation and policy evaluation. As with any set of headings, it can guide or suggest things to be looked at, in an orderly manner, when someone in government is faced with a particular policy problem. It is even possible that the results of the analysis, based on a policy cycle, may be better than without one. In methods according to the steps in analysis is more than a method or techniques. It is a way of thinking about problems, of organising data, and of presenting findings. Policy analysis develops their own styles and their personalised ways of orchestrating information. However, we believe beginning analysts can develop a set of basic skills and a general approach that will provide a foundation for analytical development. Policy-making in a federal system like ours often tends to be complex. The constitutional order sets the parameters of the policy-making process. The Constitution asserts that policy-making should be deliberative. Federalism makes sweeping national changes in policy decisions more arduous lengthy constitution and the maze of laws are mainly responsible for litigation as well as slowness with regard to policy making and implementation.

To wind up this discussion, it can be noted that the field of Public Policy has assumed considerable importance in response to the increasing complexity of the society. The study of Public Policy helps us to understand the social ills of the subject under study. Public Policy is an important mechanism for moving a social system from the past to the future.

CHAPTER TWO

Decentralization

Introduction

Decentralization is a concept which can be defined as transfer or dispersal of decision making powers, accompanied by delegation of authority to individuals or units at all levels of an organization, even if any are located far away from the power centre. In the context of power and governance, decentralization signifies the devolution of power and authority of governance of central and state governments to the sub-state level organisations i.e., Panchayats and Municipal Corporations in India.

In brief, Decentralization can be defined as the organizational structure. In such a structure, the top management of a firm entrusts the middle and lower-level management with the responsibility to take decisions pertaining to the firm's daily operations.

To elaborate, they are responsible for planning, crafting suitable strategies and taking necessary decisions to boost the proficiency at each level and in turn, optimizing the overall productivity of the company.

Owing to its numerous benefits and positive influence on the company's performance, business owners tend to prioritize the structure of power delegation. Resultantly, they can make the most of the time and opportunity to focus on the major concerns of their business and also to plan its expansion.

In the era of globalisation, where the entire world is connected and turned into a small village, decentralisation is a development process facilitating development ideas that are pro-poor, pro-nature and protects the regional characteristics in the development process. This process will help in bringing out the voice of the depressed, poorest of the poor and make decisions that are democratic and also help in the representation of the local communities in the decision making process.

Meaning

Decentralization denotes dispersal of authority among a number of individual or unit. The root of the English word decentralization can be traced back to a Latin word, which means away from the centre.

L.D. White defined decentralization as the process of transfer of administrative power from a higher to a lower level of organization.

Henry Fayol states that everything that goes to increase the role of subordinate is decentralization and everything that goes to reduce it is centralization. However, it is very difficult to pin down the exact meaning of the term decentralization as the concept is often confused with similar ideas like deconcentration, devolution, delegation and privatization. In deconcentration, a superior officer lessens his workload by delegating some of his functions to his subordinate so that administration functions efficiently and effectively. Devolution, which also implies dispersal of authority, is a process wherein power is transferred from one organ of government to another by means of legislations or constitution.

Decentralization is also different from delegation. Delegation means entrusting part of one's work to others. Decentralization, on the other hand, is much broader concept. It is transfer of planning, decision making or administrative authority from the central government to its field organizations, local administrations units, semi-autonomous and parastatals organizations, local governments or NGOs. The basic idea of decentralization is therefore sharing the decision-making authority with lower levels in organisations, thereby improving their efficiency, effectiveness and responsiveness.

Types of Decentralization

Types of Decentralization

Decentralization takes different form in different political setting and administrative conditions. There are four types of decentralization. These are: political, administrative, fiscal and functional decentralization.

1. Political Decentralization

Political decentralization refers to processes where the power of political decision making and central functions are transferred from higher level of government to lower one. The institutions which are assigned authority and functions for local governance are governed by local people. Thus, the people residing in the periphery of local institution have greater chances of participation in decision making. Greater participation of people leads to increased legitimacy and more political stability of governments. Also mass participation makes for better policy making and effective utilization of resources. Seventy third and seventy fourth constitutional amendment is landmark piece of legislation for setting up three tiers rural and urban governance is extension of political decentralization.

In other words, it is the transfer of political authority and devolution of powers to the low levels of administration that are below the center. For example, the transfer of power to the states and district authorities from the center is a form of political decentralization.

2. Administrative Decentralization

It is the transfer of power to make decisions that involve utilization of natural resources, mobilization of other resources, administrative authority. It is again divided into divestment, devolution and deconcentration. Divestment is when the powers are transferred to some voluntary organizations from the government. A delegation is an exclusive form in which the powers and authority are delegated to the subordinate officials.

Administrative decentralization occurs when a politically independent unit delegates some of its power and function to subordinate units within its organisation. Administrative decentralization may be territorial or functional. Territorial decentralization means creation of area administrative units such as Divisions, District, Zones, Circles etc. and vesting them with authority and responsibility in prescribed limits.

3. Fiscal Decentralization

It is the devolution of economic powers to the lower rungs. This is again divided into two elements. One is devolution of power to spend the money and allotting them with some funds. Another element is to allow the lower levels to collect revenue in the form of taxes and cess charges.

Fiscal Decentralization means devolution of financial power to lower level of government. Unless the power to tax and generate revenue is granted, the political decentralization would merely remain a dream. The local government cannot fulfil their responsibility in the absence of adequate financial power. For instance there is provision of State Finance Commission in the seventy third and seventy forth constitutional amendment acts to review the financial position of local bodies and to suggest measure to strengthen their financial position. One of the reasons why Panchayati Raj could not succeed is inadequate financial power. The Status Report (2000) on the Autonomy of Panchayati Raj Institutions and Municipal Bodies reveals that none of the states in India, except Kerala, have tried to place requisites for financial decentralization, while operationalizing their respective acts.

4. Functional Decentralization

Functional decentralization refers to the transfer of functions from Central or state government to local bodies in order to enable them to discharge assigned functions and responsibilities. For instance seventy third constitutional amendment acts in India assigns 29 functions to Panchayati Raj intuitions in India listed in Eleventh Schedule of Constitution of India. However, these are suggestive not mandatory as under the Indian Constitution local government is state subject. Subjects and activities assigned to local bodies under functional decentralization should be precise and clear or it can create more confusion and chaos rather than empowerment of local community as it happens in most of states in India. The same applies to urban local bodies which are assigned eighteen functions by 12th schedule of Constitution of India.

Features of Decentralization in India

Reservation provision exists for the SC, ST, women and OBC at times. This reservation is extended to panchayat level administration also.

Article 243E of the Indian constitution clearly mentions forming local level panchayats and also makes a provision to constitute the next panchayat before the completion of its term.

The constitution also recognizes that the panchayats need some powers to function and made a provision making the state government devolution some powers to the panchayats.

Importance of Decentralization

Now that we have gained a basic idea about decentralization. Let's glance through its vital role in a commercial set-up mentioned below –

1. Accelerates Decision Making

Since middle and lower-level management is in charge of everyday operations, it accelerates the process of decision making. The freedom to take prompt decisions further enables them to execute their decisions quickly and effectively.

2. Improves Leadership Skills

As employees have the freedom to perform tasks individually, it offers them substantial exposure. In turn, it helps to create a work environment; wherein, employees can hone their executive skills significantly. As they learn to improve their skills and take responsibility for various tasks, it enhances the overall productivity of the firm.

3. Improves Administration

As the manager at each level is allowed to make decisions pertaining to their department, it offers them more room to bring necessary adjustments through the course of operation. In turn, it not only helps to improve the quality of the department's performance as and when required but also allows them to come up with suitable solutions to tackle departmental challenges. All of this helps to improve the quality of administration at each level significantly.

4. Facilitates Greater Control

With the help of decentralization, top management can evaluate the performance of different departments more effectively. Further, it helps them to review and identify the prevailing shortcomings and helps to bring necessary changes to the same. This not just helps to lower the occurrence of operational shortcomings but also offers greater control over each area of operation.

Significance of decentralization

Participation and control of governance by the people of the country is the essence of democracy. Such participation is possible only when the powers of the state are decentralised to the districts, block and village levels where all the sections of the people can sit together to discuss their problems as well as monitor the implementation of the programmes. Decentralization is a prime mechanism through which democracy becomes truly representative and responsive. Mohit Bhattacharya argues that the latest thinking on decentralization veers around power equalization and participation.

Organization theory and political science, which did not meet very often in the past have now almost come together in explaining the concept of decentralization. G. Shabbir Cheema and Dennis A. Rondenilli have identified the following advantages of decentralization:

(a) It provides relief to the higher officials by reducing their workload. Thus, the top executive can devote greater time and energy to important policy matters. It provides opportunity for people's participation in administration which strengthens the democracy by making it realistic and comprehensive.

(b) It increases the morale and motivations of employees particularly at lower and middle levels by assigning them authority and responsibility for different work.

(c) Decentralization could allow better political and administrative penetration of national government policies into the remote areas.

Advantages of Decentralization

Moving on, let's quickly check out how a firm benefits through decentralization –

1. Facilitates Smooth Communication

With the presence of fewer hierarchical levels, there is a smooth flow of communication between the superiors and subordinates in each department. In turn, such a set-up comes in handy for the top management and keeps them informed about the grievances and functioning of each department.

Additionally, it allows them to reach out to their subordinates as and when required and implement decisions more effectively.

2. Promotes Expansion

With the middle and lower-level management being more involved with the everyday operation, the top management seeks the opportunity to focus on expansion and sustenance of profitability.

Further, with decentralization management is more adept at identifying areas that require more attention or reforms to emerge as more productive. This helps management to make necessary changes quickly and with more effect, thus facilitating expansion and profitability in a real sense.

3. Motivates Subordinates

Decentralization is an effective way to boost the morale and feeling of job satisfaction among employees. Being entrusted with responsibilities around the department offers them a sense of belonging and further inculcates a team spirit in them.

Although decentralization lays a positive impact on the productivity of a firm, it brings forth specific challenges as well.

Disadvantages of Decentralization

Take note of these common challenges of a decentralized firm –

1. External factors

Factors like market fluctuations, government policies and intervention and trade union movement often present a challenge to optimize the productivity of a company through decentralization.

2. Lack of coordination

Each department is given due powers to delegate their operations adequately. However, different departments may not be eager to cooperate, which defeats the purpose of a decentralized structure altogether.

Approaches to Decentralization

In Political Science and Public Administration decentralization has been discussed basically from the view point of arrangement of Government. James W. Fasler has grouped the different approaches to decentralization into four categories. These are: the doctrinal, the political, the administrative and the dual role.

1) Doctrinal approach- This approach seeks to treat decentralization as an end in itself instead of treating it as a means to achieve organizational efficiency and effectiveness. This approach lays stress on the empowerment of local community – the city, town or village. In India, the Panchayati Raj supposedly embodies an ancient tradition of local autonomy. The essence of this approach is people empowerment by granting them decision making and functional authority. Thus, this approach instead of treating decentralization as a means to the achievement of some end–values, considers it as an end in itself.

2) The political approach- This approach believes that decentralization occurs in a political setting. The will to create decentralized units and granting them necessary authority for their autonomous functioning is politically decided. To create and maintain local government is, thus, a major political commitment.

In the absence of such commitment, it will merely remain in law than in actual practice. Fesler pointed out illusory decentralization. For example in India although devolution of power to local bodies have been granted formally but these bodies are not given funds, functions and functionaries essential to operate as an autonomous institution and are strongly controlled or influenced by respective state governments.

3) The administrative approach- This approach is based on the principle of efficiency and effectiveness. When field administrative units are set-up through a process of decentralization, the measure is suitable for field level decision making and for redressal of grievances. In this process, many administrative units might come up between the local administration and the Central Headquarters. Currently, district administration in India is faced with these problems of area function duality. To resolve this problem and to promote such operational principles conscious attempts are needed to readjust from time to time conflicting claims of area and function in deconcentrated field administration.

4) The dual role approach- The dual approach seeks to highlight the conflict in field administration between tradition and change. The basic conflict, according to Fesler, is between the traditional function of maintenance of law and order and advancement of socio-economic development. The main function of administration was to maintain law and order and collection of revenue. However, the changed concept of welfare state requires rapid socio-economic development. It demands cooperation and participation of people in administration and increased coordination among different administrative units. Thus there is urgent need to change the system into decentralized, participative and innovative one. The resolution of conflict between two different orientations in the field administration calls for adaptations of decentralization to changing circumstances.

Decentralization is favoured for access, citizen participation and political responsiveness. Therefore, decentralization depends on the situation and is not an absolute term. The four approaches of W. Fasler address different issues and challenges in the realization of decentralization. The doctrinal approach treats decentralization as an end in itself. The political approach highlights political character of decentralization. The administrative approach is based on efficiency, effectiveness and rationality. Finally, the reorientation of roles from status quo to change orientation is the crux of dual role approach.

Conclusion

In the foregoing analysis, an attempt has been made to situate the forms of decentralization. Decentralization is favoured for access, citizen participation and political responsiveness. Therefore, decentralization depends on the situation and is not an absolute term. These four types show how decentralization takes different form in different political setting and administrative conditions.

Local Self Governance: Rural and Urban
Introduction

It is almost 30 years since the 73rd and 74th Constitutional Amendment Acts, creating the new Local Governance Framework in India, were made operational in April 1993. The Acts, focused on enabling democratic decentralization, have provisions that devolved a range of powers and responsibilities to local elected bodies and made them accountable to the people for their implementation. The new system of local governance has proved to be remarkably beneficial in some aspects. Yet, there are some lacunae, especially in the implementation of several provisions, which has limited the effectiveness of these reforms.

Oxford Dictionary defines local self governance as the system of government of a town or an area by elected representatives of the people who live there.

Merriam Webster Dictionary defines self government as the act of governing one's self or the state of being governed by one's self; self-control; self-command.

Evolution of Local Governance in India

There is long evolutionary history of local governance in India. Evidence from the Rig-Veda (1700 BC) shows self-governing village organisations called Sabhas. In time, these bodies became panchayats (council of five). The decentralization of authority was present in the Mauryan to Gupta dynasties. The British also tried to establish decentralized systems, albeit with very little powers. The Royal Commission on Decentralization (1907) under the chairmanship of Sir H.W. Primrose recognized the importance of panchayats at the village level. Under the Government of India Act, 1935 Provincial Governments were responsible for local governance. They enacted legislations but little powers were provided to Panchayats.

The framers of the Constitution of India included Article 40 among the Directive Principles: "The state shall organise village panchayats and endow them with such powers and authority as may be necessary to enable them to function as units of self-government". Four committees (between 1957 to 1986) conceptualised local self-government in India; Balwant Rai Mehta Committee (1957), the Ashok Mehta Committee (1977–1984), GVK Rao Committee (1985) and the LM Singhvi Committee (1986).

Eventually, the local Governance was given Constitutional Status with the 73rd/74th Constitutional Amendment Acts in 1992. The Amendment Acts of 1992 added two new parts IX and IX-A to the Constitution. Two new Schedules 11 and 12 were also added which contain the lists of functional items of Panchayats and Municipalities.

What is the structure of Local Governance in India?

The 73rd/74th Amendment Acts established a three-tier system of Panchayati Raj in every state – at the village, intermediate and district levels.

For rural areas, there are three nested bodies. At the top is the District Council or Zilla Parishad, which is made up of a cluster of Block Councils or Panchayat Samitis, which in turn are made up of village councils or Gram Panchayats. Each village has a village assembly or gram sabha comprising all adults in the village. Gram Sabha has the power to directly elect members of the panchayat. States with a population of less than two million may choose to have a two-tiered structure without the intermediate block-level institution.

In urban areas, there are three types of local bodies: Municipal Corporations (Mahanagar Palikas for areas with a population of more than one million), Municipal Councils/Municipalities (Nagar Palikas for areas with less than a million people) and Town Councils (Nagar Panchayats for areas transitioning from rural to urban).

Scheduled and Tribal areas are legally exempt from implementing the Panchayati Raj system. The Panchayat Extension to Scheduled Areas (PESA) Act, 1996 provides for the extension of the 73rd Amendment (with certain modifications and exceptions) to tribal and forested areas across 10 states of India (excluding tribal areas in the states of Assam, Meghalaya, Tripura and Mizoram which are governed by District or Regional Councils). These provisions have been put in place to protect customary law, social and religious practices and traditional management practices of community resources.

A minimum of one-third of the seats in all local bodies are reserved for women. Seats are also reserved for people belonging to scheduled castes, scheduled tribes and other backward classes in proportion to their population.

What are the roles of Panchayati Raj Institution (PRIs)/Local Governance Bodies?

PRIs play a crucial role in rural development and perform the following roles:

(a) Administrative activities such as the maintenance of village records, the construction, maintenance and repair of roads, tanks, wells and so on;

(b) Improving socio-economic welfare through the promotion of rural industries, health, education, women and child welfare, among others;

(c) Judicial functions such as trying petty civil and criminal cases such as minor thefts and money disputes are also performed either by separate adalati or nyaya panchayats or by gram panchayats.

What are the challenges in working of Local Government Bodies?

Functional Challenges:

The power to devolve functions to local governments rests with the State Government. Most States have not devolved adequate functions to local government bodies. This has severely affected the system's efficiency and effectiveness. State Governments have created parallel structures for the implementation of projects around agriculture, health and education, which undermines the status of local bodies. Local bodies lack the support systems necessary to carry out their mandates. The 74th amendment requires a District Planning Committee to be set up in each district, so that the development plans prepared by the panchayats and urban local bodies can be consolidated and integrated. According to a study by the India Development Review (IDR, a think tank), District Planning Committees are non-functional in 9 states and failed to prepare integrated plans in 15 states.

Financial Challenges:

(a) Local government expenditure as a percentage of GDP is only 2%. This is extremely low compared to other major economies like China (11%) and Brazil (7%);

(b) Most local bodies, both rural and urban are unable to generate adequate funds from their internal sources and are therefore extremely dependent on external sources for funding. Studies show that around 80-95% of revenue is obtained from external sources, particularly State and Union Government loans and grants;

(c) The volume of money set apart for them is inadequate to meet their basic requirements. Local Governments are starved of resources. The Union Finance Commissions have made desirable recommendations, but the actual devolution of funds has been very poor. Not more than 5% of the divisible pool of Union taxes is given to local governments;

(d) The devolution of funds is associated with conditionalities that bind them to specific uses. (i.e., top driven schemes of Union/State Governments, rather than based on local needs). The Government-appointed officers have complete control over spending of funds instead of the elected representatives of local governments;

(e) State Finance Commissions are not established as per Constitutional requirements (constitute every 5 years). By 2014-15, States should have created 5th State Finance Commission (SFC) in their respective States, but only 13 had created them. By 2019, when 6th State Finance Commission should have been constituted, some States were yet to create 3rd or 4th Commissions. J&K had created only 1 SFC by April 2019;

(f) Some experts argue that Local governments are reluctant to collect property taxes and user charges because of fear of backlash from public. They are happy to implement top-down programmes because they know that if they collect taxes, their electoral prospects will be hampered.

Functionary Challenges:

(a) Every local government needs to have organisational capacity, by way of staff such as office and clerical staff and social mobilisers. Staffing of local governments is scanty. Many panchayats share a single secretary, who is often overburdened;

(b) Technology has been used to centralize the delivery of local services which has been detrimental to local decision-making.

Other Challenges:

(a) Criminal elements and contractors are attracted to local government elections especially in urban areas. They are able to win elections through corrupt means as local elections do not get same scrutiny as State Assembly or General Elections;

(b) Elections to the local bodies are often delayed. For long period of times there are no functional local governments;

(c) Despite a relatively higher level of literacy and educational standard, city-dwellers do not take adequate interest in the functioning of the urban government bodies e.g., the turnout in Municipal Elections in Delhi and Mumbai in 2017 was only 53% and 55% respectively;

(d) While women have been empowered with representation through reservation of seats, the 'Sarpanch Pati' syndrome limits the effectiveness. ('Sarpanch Pati' syndrome: Women Sarpanch is only nominal head, the male relative (generally husband) wield actual power).

What steps can be taken going ahead?

First, the provisions of 73rd/74th Constitutional Amendments should be implemented in true spirit. State Finance Commissions should be regularly constituted with clearly defined Terms of Reference (ToR). ToR should include recommendation to devolve more funds and make the functioning of local bodies more effective. Adequate powers to raise own revenues should be devolved to local governments.

Second, the elections should be held at regular intervals without any delay. State Governments and State Election Commissions must be held accountable for delays.

Third, Gram Sabhas and wards committees (in urban areas) have to be revitalized. Consultations with the grama sabha could be organised through smaller discussions where everybody can participate to make them inclusive. New media of communication like social media groups could be used for facilitating discussions between members of a grama sabha/ward committees.

Fourth, local government organisational structures have to be strengthened. Panchayats are burdened with a huge amount of work that other departments thrust on them without being compensated for the extra administrative costs. Local governments must be enabled to hold State departments accountable and to provide quality, corruption free service to them.

Fifth, there is a need to improve capabilities of human resources through training, process consultation, action research methods and workshops.

Sixth, citizen participation and engagement in local governance can be enhanced with the help of NGOs and civil society organizations. Citizens also need to be informed about the functioning and consequences of decisions taken by the local government bodies. The general public also need to be informed about the role of the service providers, the cost of services, the sources of their financing etc.

Conclusion

Empowering the local bodies for Local Governance has been one of the most progressive reform since Independence. It has envisioned to place the governing power in the hands of the general populace. Just like every other reform, this one has a few loopholes in it. Nevertheless, if these gaps are removed, the present local governance system can truly empower the citizens and support the inclusive growth.

Origin and Development of Local Governments in India

In tracing the origin and development of local governments in India, one finds the evidences of the existence of local governments even before the times of Christ (BCE). The period between 600 BCE to C.E. 600 witnessed the rise and fall of republics. During this period, there emerged Mahavira (founder of Jainism) and Buddha (founder of Buddhism). Villages were classified according to size and mode of habitation in Jain and Buddhists literature.

The religious orders founded by Buddha and Mahavira observed highly democratic procedures in arriving at decisions. Kautilya's Arthshastra (Treatise) gives a comprehensive account of the system of village administration prevailing in his time. In the days of Maurya, the village and the district were units of administration.

In the South Indian peninsula, the existence of the local self governing institutions could be traced well before the period of the Christian calender. The historical period can be grouped in to early Chola period, Kalabira period and the later Chola period, the emergence of Vijayanagara empire, entry of Muslims and Moghuls and the British. There were very little evidence available about the system of local governance in the early Chola Period (which dates back to Before Christ) and the Kalabira Period.

But there were some account of existence of local governments during the times of Pandyas (rulers of deep south India) and the Pallavas (rulers of mid south india). But Cholas (rulers who ruled mid Tamil country) period witnessed a well developed local self governments. The inscriptions of Paranthaka Chola – I (919.C.E. – 922.C.E.) from Utthiramerur in Kanchipuram district of Tamil Nadu state give detailed account of local self government. They inform that each village had an assembly consisting of all adult males and their involvement in general matters. These assemblies are of two types: the "Ur" and the "Mahasabha". The third kind was the nagaram (town) confined to mercantile towns (trading centers) and the fourth was the "nadu". Hence two types of institutions were mentioned one nadu (village and other areas) and nagaram (urban centers).

In general there is little information on the functioning of any village assemblies prior to the 9th century. Both "nadu" and "Nagaram" were concerned about the control and regulation of land holdings, management of irrigation works, temples, collection and remission of taxes, floating of loans for capital works and the management of charitable institutions. The "ur" and the "mahasabha" were the two institutions that assisted the officers in executing the orders of the king.

It has been found that Raja Raja Chola, the First, ordered the "mahasabha" of the Viranarayana Chaturvedi Mangalam to confiscate the property of traitors. Many historians such as Sir Charles Metcalfe, Sir George Bird wood and Eliphinstone opined that a strong system of local government existed in Ancient and medieval South India. But doubts are expressed by some of the historians about the elaborate existence of the local self government in ancient and medieval South India.

During the Moghul period A.D. (C.E.) 1500 to A.D. (C.E.) 1777, the fundamental principles of central local relationships hardly changed with change of kingdoms. When the Mughal Empire was at its zenith of glory, it was divided into provinces (Subhas) and Provinces into sub divisions (Sarkars) and Sakars into union of villages (Paraganas). At each level, the government is organized and the officials were appointed by the Emperor. In the Twilight of the Mughul Empire, the self governing institutions in rural areas had been severely damaged at vital points, but they had withstood the onslaughts with remarkable tactics.

After the Battle of Plassey in A.D. (C.E.) 1757, the British East India Company derived land taxing rights (Diwani rights) from Bengal ruler (Nawab), which was the first step in the ascendency of the British rule in India. The rural and the other urban trading centers during the British East India company rule was not under any control or supervision, except the three Presidency towns of Calcutta, Bombay and Madras. The District administration under the charge of the district collector was the king pin in the British control over vast rural areas.

The important mile stone during the company rule was the establishment of the Municipal Corporations as mentioned earlier at Calcutta (Kolkata), Bombay (Mumbai) and Madras (Chennai). Viceroy Lord Rippon in 1882 brought out a resolution proposing a smaller unit for constituting rural local boards, a sub division, tehsil (taluk) and district boards to supervise.

Lord Rippon's resolution emphasized that the institutions he proposed should have a majority of non-officials who should be elected wherever it was feasible. Nearly 500 rural boards were created with a two third majority of non officials who depended upon the district magistrate (district collector) for the favour of nomination. The main activities of the district boards till 1909 were police, public works, education and village sanitation.

The rural local government introduced by Lord Rippon faced many criticisms and in the A.D. (C.E.) 1907, the British government appointed a commission to enquire into the question of administrative and financial relations between the Government of India, Provincial governments and subordinate authorities under them so as to simplify and improve the prevalent system through devolution or otherwise. With the passing of Government of India Act, 1919, the local governments were entrusted with the elected elements of the provincial government under the diarchy system of government.

The number of the village bodies in Tamil Nadu increased from 1417 in 1926 to 6250 in 1937. There are three tier system of rural local bodies viz; District Boards, Taluk Boards and Village Boards. The District and Taluk boards have undergone changes by 1923, the non-official chairman in all provinces replaced official chairman. In Tamilnadu, most of the District Boards came to be dominated by Justice Party members which stood at 545 in 1927. From 1937 upto 1947, the rural local authorities faced many challenges including the national freedom movement.

After Indian Independence in 1947, an attempt was made to revive local governments in India. Mahatma Gandhi argued for the decentralized administrative system in India entrusting responsibility of governance with the village panchayats (self sufficient Gram Swaraj). Shrima Naryan with blessings of Gandhiji published a blue print of the Gandhian Constitution for Free India wherein panchayats are the basic institutions for organizing social, economic and political activities of the citizens. In addition to the civic, political and administrative roles, the Panchayat was to play the economic role of organizing production and distributing resources in such a way that the village communities became self sufficient for meeting most of their basic needs.

Thus Article 40 came to be incorporated in the Constitution as part of the Directive Principles of the State policy (Part –IV) of the Constitution of India adopted on Nov. 26th 1949. The Art. 40 States that, "the state shall take steps to organize village panchayats and endow them with such powers and authority as may be necessary to enable them to function as units of self government."

In compliance with the provisions of the Directive Principles of the State Policy, an ambitious rural sector initiative, the Community Development Programme was launched in 1952 with main focus of securing social-economic transformations of village through people's own democratic and cooperative organizations with the government providing technical services, supply and credit. This programme was extended to most of the blocks as National Extensions Service aimed at transferring scientific and technical knowledge to agricultural, animal husbandry and rural craft sectors. In 1956, under the Second Five Year Plan (1956- 1961), it was recommended that village panchayats should organically link with popular organizations at higher levels and in stages, the popular body should take over the whole administration. In 1957, Government of India appointed a Committee on Plan Projects under the Chairmanship of Balwant Rai Mehta. The Mehta Committee recommended two points namely, the administration should be decentralized and the administration should be placed under the control of local bodies.

Secondly, the community development blocks should be designed as administrative democratic units with an elected Panchayat Union to operate as a fulcrum of developmental activity in the area. It also recommended for the formation of District Development Councils (Zila Parishad) at the district level consisting of all the Presidents of the Panchayat Unions (Samities), Member of legislative assemblies and Members of Parliament with district level officers of the public health, agriculture, veterinary and education departments as members and the collector as the chairman. The district body is only an advisory body. The recommendation of the Mehta Committee were generally welcomed and Panchayati Raj legislations were enacted and by 1960s about 90 per cent of the population were covered by the Panchayati Raj bodies.

In 1977, the Government of India formed a committee under the chairmanship of Ashoka Mehta to go in to the working of the Panchayati Raj bodies and suggest measures to strengthen it. It recommended that Panchayati Raj should emerge as the system of democratic local government, discharging developmental, municipal and ultimate regulatory functions. Hence the first recommendation was to set up district Panchayat (Zilla Parishad) as the directly elected body. As a temporary arrangement, the committee recommended continuation of the Panchayat union at the block level. Not as a unit of local self government but as a nominated middle level support arm for the District Development Council. The Ashoka Mehta Committee submitted it's report in 1978, which was well received and led many states to introduce appropriate amendments in their Panchayat Acts such Karnataka, Maharastra, Andhra Pradesh, West Bengal and Gujarat.

A number of committees were formed between 1978 and 1986 to look into various aspects of strengthening the local self government institutions such as C.H. Hanumantha Rao Committee, G.V.K. Rao Committee and L.M. Singhvi Committee. Only minor changes were suggested by these committees from the Ashok Mehta committee. The next land mark was the introduction of 64th and 65th Constitutional Amendment Bills in July 1989 by Rajiv Gandhi government which could not be passed in the Council of States (Rajya Sabha).

After many attempts, in 1992, incorporating important features of earlier exercises on this subject, government drafted and introduced the 73rd and 74th Constitutional Amendment bills in Parliament in 1992 which was passed by the Indian Parliament in 1993. The 73rd and 74th Constitutional Amendments introduced new parts IX and IXA in the Indian Constitution containing Articles 243 to 243 ZG.

The Importance of Local Self Government in India

The success of democracy depends on the decentralization of power. Through this system of local self-government, people can obtain their democratic rights. Through this system, power can be properly decentralized and every individual can get the scope to develop his or her personality fully and properly.

The local self-governmental institutions are the best centers for imparting democratic thoughts and education. People prefer democracy because they want to live in an environment of equality and liberty.

The local self-government creates that scope for enjoying democracy. It is through these local self-governments that the local problems can be considered and solved adequately and properly. It also reduces the heavy responsibilities of the central and the state governments and establishes democracy in a wider context.

Since the members of the local self-government are local people, they can realize and understand the gravity of local problems more seriously than the administrators of the State or Central government and can properly solve them.

In local self government, the members have close and intimate contact with the local people. Naturally, it remains rather free from corruption and acts with real social welfare motif.

To implement various economic planning in local and regional levels, the local self-government institutions are far more helpful than the state or central government. It also inspires the local people to actively participate in various governmental activities.

The local self government generally unites the people with democracy and encourages them to participate in its activities without any bias or prejudice. Naturally, it can consolidate the political values and faith of ordinary people and thereby influences the political activities and political culture of the people.

Moreover, both the central and the state governments can make various administrative experiments through these local self-governments.

It thus, enables the ordinary people to take part or make active participation in the lowest level of administration. Naturally, the political socialization of local people becomes possible.

Moreover, the local self-government is conducive to equality and liberty and the perfect medium for satisfying the needs and grievances of the people at local and regional level.

Basic Features of 73ʳᵈ Constitutional Amendment Act

The 73ʳᵈ Amendment 1992 added a new Part IX to the constitution titled "The Panchayats" covering provisions from Article 243 to 243(O) and a new Eleventh Schedule covering 29 subjects within the functions of the Panchayats.

Significance of the amendment

This amendment implements the Article 40 of the DPSP which says that "State shall take steps to organise village panchayats and endow them with such powers and authority as may be necessary to enable them to function as units of self-government" and have upgraded them from non-justifiable to justifiable part of the constitution and has put constitutional obligation upon states to enact the Panchayati Raj Acts as per provisions of the Part IX. However, states have been given enough freedom to take their geographical, politico-administrative and others conditions into account while adopting the Panchayati Raj System.

Salient Features

a) Gram Sabha

Gram Sabha is a body consisting of all the persons registered in the electoral rolls relating to a village comprised within the area of Panchayat at the village level. Since all the persons registered in electoral rolls are members of Gram Sabha, there are no elected representatives. Further, Gram Sabha is the only permanent unit in Panchayati Raj system and not constituted for a particular period. Although it serves as foundation of the Panchayati Raj, yet it is not among the three tiers of the same. The powers and functions of Gram Sabha are fixed by state legislature by law.

b) Three Tiers of Panchayati Raj

Part IX provides for a 3 tier Panchayat system, which would be constituted in every state at the village level, intermediate level and district level. This provision brought the uniformity in the Panchayati Raj structure in India. However, the states which were having population below 20 lakh were given an option to not to have the intermediate level.

All the members of these three level are elected. Further, the chairperson of panchayats at the intermediate and district levels are indirectly elected from amongst the elected members. But at the village level, the election of chairperson of Panchayat (Sarpanch) may be direct or indirect as provided by the state in its own Panchayati Raj Act.

c) Reservation in Panchayats

There is a provision of reservation of seats for SCs and STs at every level of Panchayat. The seats are to be reserved for SCs and STs in proportion to their population at each level. Out of the Reserved Seats, 1/3ʳᵈ have to be reserved for the women of the SC and ST. Out of the total number of seats to be filled by the direct elections, 1/3ʳᵈ have to be reserved for women. There has been an amendment bill pending that seeks to increase reservation for women to 50%. The reserved seats may be allotted by rotation to different constituencies in the Panchayat. The State by law may also provide for reservations for the offices of the Chairpersons.

d) Duration of Panchayats

A clear term for 5 years has been provided for the Panchayats and elections must take place before the expiry of the terms. However, the Panchayat may be dissolved earlier on specific grounds in accordance with the state legislations. In that case the elections must take place before expiry of 6 months of the dissolution.

e) Disqualification of Members

Article 243F makes provisions for disqualifications from the membership. As per this article, any person who is qualified to become an MLA is qualified to become a member of the Panchayat, but for Panchayat the minimum age prescribed is 21 years. Further, the disqualification criteria are to be decided by the state legislature by law.

f) Finance Commission

State Government needs to appoint a finance commission every five years, which shall review the financial position of the Panchayats and to make recommendation on the following:

• The Distribution of the taxes, duties, tolls, fees, etc. levied by the state which is to be divided between the Panchayats.

• Allocation of proceeds between various tiers.

• Taxes, tolls, fees assigned to Panchayats.

• Grant in aids.

This report of the Finance Commission would be laid on the table in the State legislature. Further, the Union Finance Commission also suggests the measures needed to augment the Consolidated Funds of States to supplement the resources of the panchayats in the states.

g) Powers and Functions: 11th Schedule

The state legislatures are needed to enact laws to endow powers and authority to the Panchayats to enable them functions of local government. The 11th schedule enshrines the distribution of powers between the State Legislature and the Panchayats. These 29 subjects are listed below:

11th Schedule of the Constitution

1. Agriculture, including agricultural extension.
2. Land improvement, implementation of land reforms, land consolidation and soil conservation.
3. Minor irrigation, water management and watershed development.
4. Animal husbandry, dairying and poultry.
5. Fisheries.
6. Social forestry and farm forestry.
7. Minor forest produce.
8. Small scale industries, including food processing industries.
9. Khadi, village and cottage industries.
10. Rural housing.
11. Drinking water.
12. Fuel and fodder.
13. Roads, culverts, bridges, ferries, waterways and other means of communication.
14. Rural electrification, including distribution of electricity.
15. Non-conventional energy sources.
16. Poverty alleviation programme.
17. Education, including primary and secondary schools.
18. Technical training and vocational education.
19. Adult and non-formal education.
20. Libraries.
21. Cultural activities.
22. Markets and fairs.
23. Health and sanitation, including hospitals, primary health centers and dispensaries.

24. Family welfare.

25. Women and child development.

26. Social welfare, including welfare of the handicapped and mentally retarded.

27. Welfare of the weaker sections and in particular of the Scheduled Castes and the Scheduled Tribes.

28. Public distribution system.

29. Maintenance of community assets.

Further, the state legislature can authorize the Panchayats to collect and appropriate suitable local taxes and provide grant in aids to the Panchayats from the Consolidated Funds of the states.

h) Audit of Accounts

State Government can make provisions for audit of accounts of the Panchayats.

i) Elections

Article 243K enshrines the provisions with respect to elections of the Panchayats. This article provides for constitution of a State Election Commission in respect of the Panchayats. This State Election Commission would have the power to supervise, direct and control the elections to the Panchayats and also prepare the electoral rolls.

The article maintains the independence of the election commission by making provisions that the election commissioner of this commissioner would be removed only by manner and on same grounds as a Judge of the High Court.

If there is a dispute in the Panchayat elections, the Courts have no jurisdiction over them. This means that the Panchayat election can be questioned only in the form of an election petition presented to an authority which the State Legislature by law can prescribe.

Important

The election commissioner for this reason is to be appointed by the Governor. The terms and conditions of the office of the Election commissioners have also to be decided by the Governor.

j) Applications to Union Territories

Provisions of Panchayats shall be applicable to the UTs in same way as in case of the states but the President by a public notification may make any modifications in the applications of any part.

k) Exempted areas and states

The provisions of part IX are not applicable to the following:

• Entire states of Nagaland, Meghalaya and Mizoram

• Hill areas in the State of Manipur for which District Councils

• Further, the district level provisions shall not apply to the hill areas of the District of Darjeeling in the State of West Bengal which affect the Darjeeling Gorkha Hill Council.

• The reservation provisions are not applicable to Arunachal Pradesh.

Continuance of Existing Laws

Any provision of any law relating to Panchayats in force in a State immediately before the commencement of the Constitution (Seventy-third Amendment) Act, 1992, which is inconsistent with the provisions of this Part, shall continue to be in force until amended or repealed by a competent legislature or competent authority.

Bar on Interference by Courts

Article 243 O bars the courts to interfere in the Panchayat Matters. The validity of any law relating to the delimitation of constituencies or the allotment of seats to such constituencies cannot be questioned in a court. No election to any Panchayat is to be questioned except by an election petition presented to such authority and in such manner as provided by the state legislature.

Comment

The positive impact of the 73rd Amendment in rural India is clearly visible as it has changed power equations significantly. Elections to the Panchayats in most states are being held regularly. Through over 600 District Panchayats, around 6000 Intermediate Panchayats and 2.3 lakh Gram Panchayats, more than 28 lakh persons now have a formal position in our representative democracy.

Still, this bill lacks the proper definition of the role of the bureaucracy. It does not clearly define the role of the state government. On practical level, people are illiterate in India and they are actually not aware of these novel features. The Panchayats are dominated by effluents in some parts of the country. The 3 tiers of the Panchayati Raj have still very limited financial powers and their viability is entirely dependent upon the political will of the states.

Salient features of 74th amendment act

Classification of municipalities: The act provides for the constitution of the following three-types of municipalities in every state - Nagar panchayat, municipal council and municipal corporation.

Composition:

All members of the municipality should be elected directly by the people.

For this purpose, each municipal area shall be divided into territorial constituencies known was wards.

The state legislature is empowcred to provide for the manner of election of the chairperson of a municipality.

The state legislature can also provide for representation of persons having special knowledge who will not have the right to vote in the meeting, members of LS, RS, state legislature and council from the municipal area.

The chairpersons of the committees other than wards committee.

Wards Committees:

Article 243S of the Constitution make the provisions for constitution and composition of Wards Committees, etc. consisting of one or more wards, within the territorial area of a Municipality having a population of three lakhs or more.

A member of a Municipality representing a ward within the territorial area of the Wards Committee shall be a member of that Committee. Where a Wards Committee consists of two or more wards, one of the members representing such wards in the Municipality elected by the members of the Wards Committee shall be the Chairperson of that Committee.

Reservation of seats:

Article 243T makes the provisions for the reservation of seats. Seats are reserved for the Scheduled Castes and the Scheduled Tribes in every Municipally and the number of seats so reserved shall bear, as nearly as may be, the same proportion to the total number of seats to be filled by direct election in that Municipality as the population of the Scheduled Castes in the Municipal area or of the Scheduled Tribes in the Municipal area bears to the total population of that area and such seats may be allotted by rotation to different constituencies in a Municipality.

Not less than one-third of the total number of seats reserved Scheduled Caste are reserved for women belonging to the Scheduled Castes or, as the case may be, the Scheduled Tribes.

Not less than one-third (including the number of seats reserved for women belonging to the Scheduled Castes and the Scheduled Tribes) of the total number of seats to be filled by direct election in every Municipality are reserved for women and such seats may be allotted by rotation to different constituencies in a Municipality.

The office of Chairpersons in the Municipalities shall be reserved for the Scheduled Castes, the Scheduled Tribes and women in such manner as the Legislature of a State may, by law, provide.

Duration of Municipalities:

As per Article 243U of the Constitution, every Municipality, unless sooner dissolved under any law for the time being in force, shall continue for five years from the date appointed for its first meeting and no longer provided that a Municipality shall be given a reasonable opportunity of being heard before its dissolution.

Disqualification:

A person shall be disqualified for being chosen as or for being a member of a municipality if he is so disqualified.

Under any law for the time being in force for the purpose of elections for state legislature.

Under any law made by state legislature.

However, no person shall be disqualified on the ground that he is less than 25 years of age if he has attained 21 years of age.

All questions related to this will be decided by an authority so determined by the state legislature.

State Election Commission:

The superintendence, direction and control of the preparation of electoral rolls and the conduct of all elections to the municipalities shall be vested in the state election commission.

Powers and functions:

As per Article 243W of the Constitution states the powers, authority and responsibilities of Municipalities, etc. Subject to the provisions of this Constitution, the Legislature of a State may, by law, endow:

the Municipalities with such powers and authority as may be necessary to enable them to function as institutions of self-government and such law may contain provisions for the devolution of powers and responsibilities upon Municipalities, subject to such conditions as may be specified therein, with respect to-

The preparation of plans for economic development and social justice;

The performance of functions and the implementation of schemes as may be entrusted to them including those in relation to the matters listed in the Twelfth Schedule;

The Committees with such powers and authority as may be necessary to enable them to carry out the responsibilities conferred upon them including those in relation to the matters listed in the Twelfth Schedule.

Finances:

The state legislature may

Authorize a municipality to levy, collect and appropriate taxes.

Assign to municipality taxes, levies, tolls and fees levied and collected by state government.

Provide for making grants-in-aid to the municipalities.

Provide for constitution of funds for crediting all moneys to the municipalities.

Audit of account:

The state legislature will specify the manner in which the auditing has to be done.

Application to union territories:

It shall apply with such modification and exception has the President may determine.

Exempted areas:

It does not apply to the scheduled areas and tribal areas in the states.

District planning committee:

It is the committee created as per article 243ZD. As per this, every state shall constitute at the district level, a district planning committee to consolidate the plans prepared by panchayats and municipalities in the district and to prepare a draft development plan for the district as a whole. The state legislature may make provisions with respect to the following:

Composition of such committees

Manner of election of members of such committees.

Functions of such committees in relation to district planning.

Manner of the election of the chairpersons of such committees.

The act lay down that 80% of the members of this committee will be elected by the elected members from the municipalities and panchayats in the region amongst themselves.

While preparation of the plans following areas have to be considered:

Matters of common interest between the panchayats and municipalities.

The extent and type of available resources.

Consult such institutions and organization as specified by the governor.

Metro planning committee:

As per Article 243ZE of the constitution, in every Metropolitan area, a Metropolitan Planning Committee may be constituted to prepare a draft development plan for the Metropolitan area as a whole.

The state legislature may make provisions with respect to the following:

Composition of such committees

Manner of election of members of such committees

Functions of such committees in relation to district planning

Manner of the election of the chairpersons of such committees

The act lay down that 66% of the members of this committee will be elected by the elected members from the municipalities and panchayats in the region amongst themselves.

While preparation of the plan the following things have to be kept in mind:

Plans prepared by the municipalities and panchayats

Matters of common interest between the local bodies

Overall objectives and priorities set by the GoI and government of the state

Available resources of investment

Consult such institutions as specified by the governor

The act also bars the interference of the court in electoral matters relating to municipalities. It empowers the state legislature to determine the manner in which a petition questioning the election and also to the authority as it deems fit.

Urban Local Government in India

Urbanisation has become a common feature of Indian society. With cities being the main beneficiaries of globalisation, along with increasing urban population, millions of people chasing jobs are migrating to cities.

This signifies the need to position Indian cities as drivers of the structural transformation of the Indian economy. It requires enhancement and upgradation of infrastructure which calls for active support by State Governments and also the Central Government.

Our Constitution provides a clear mandate for Democratic Decentralisation not only through the Directive Principles of State Policy but more specifically through the 73rd and 74th Amendments of the Constitution which seek to create an institutional framework for ushering in grassroot democracy through the medium of genuinely self-governing local bodies in both urban and rural areas of the country.

However, despite the constitutional mandate, the growth of self-governing local bodies as the third tier of governance in the country has been uneven and slow. The transfer of 3F (funds, functions and functionaries) has been nominal (with notable exceptions such as Kerala).

Integrating Institutional reforms in local governance with economic reforms was Gandhiji's far-sighted vision of 'Poorna Swaraj'. But Reserve Bank of India (RBI) in a report State Finances, Study of Budgets of 2021-22, released in November 2021 stated that, with the third-tier governments in India playing a frontline role in combating the pandemic by implementing containment strategies, healthcare, their finances have come under severe strain, forcing them to cut down expenditures and mobilise funding from various sources.

What is the Structure of Urban Local Government in India?

The Urban Local Government consists of eight types of Urban local bodies.

Municipal Corporation:

Municipal corporations are usually found in big cities such as Bangalore, Delhi, Mumbai, Kolkata, etc.

Municipality:

The smaller cities tend to have the provision of municipalities. The Municipalities are often called upon by other names such as the municipal council, municipal committee, municipal board, etc.

Notified Area Committee:

Notified area committees are set up for the fast-developing towns and the towns lacking the basic amenities. All the members of the notified area committee are nominated by the state government.

Town Area Committee:

The town area committee is found in the small towns. It has minimal authority such as street lighting, drainage roads, and conservancy.

Cantonment Board:

It is usually set up for a civilian population living in the cantonment area. It is created and run by the central government.

Township:

Township is another form of urban government to provide basic facilities to the staff and workers living in the colonies established near the plant. It has no elected members and is merely an extension of the bureaucratic structure.

Port Trust

Port Trusts are established in the port areas such as Mumbai, Chennai, Kolkata, etc. It manages and takes care of the port. It also provides basic civic amenities to the people living in that area.

Special Purpose Agency:

These agencies undertake the designated activities or specific functions belonging to the municipal corporations or municipalities.

What are the Problems Faced by Urban Local Bodies?

Financial Paucity:

Financial stringency has become the biggest hurdle in good governance at ground level.

Dependence on Intergovernmental Transfers:

The Urban local government heavily depends on the state governments for getting grants-in-aid out of the consolidated fund of state.

Acute Share in Revenue:

Generally, their source of income is inadequate as compared to their functions. Their chief sources of income are the varied types of taxes. However, taxes collected by the urban bodies are not sufficient to cover the expenses of the services provided. Though they can impose certain new taxes, the elected members of these local bodies hesitate in doing so for fear of displeasing their electorate.

Unplanned Urbanisation:

In absence of proper planning, the Municipal Services find it difficult to cope with the increasing needs of the population, both qualitatively and quantitatively. The administrative machinery of local bodies is insufficient. Judicious use of land is not being made, colonies are set up without proper facilities such as schools, parks and hospitals, the growth of slums is not checked, traffic congestion. This also leads to urban poverty, unemployment and ecological degradation.

Excessive Control of State Government:

The State Government takes control of the Urban local bodies which are legislative, administrative, judicial and financial keeps urban municipal governments subordinate units rather than functioning as institutions of self-governance. Municipalities need to balance their budgets by law and any municipal borrowing has to be approved by the state government.

Unlike the Centre and the States, no distinction is made between revenue expenditure and capital expenditure at the Urban Local Government level.

Multiplicity of Agencies:

Formation of single purpose agencies under the direct supervision of the state government and without any accountability towards urban local government. The municipal bodies have to contribute to the budget to these agencies while having no control over them.

Example: State Transport Corporation, State Electricity Board, Water Supply Department, etc.

Low level of People's Participation:

Despite a relatively higher level of literacy and educational standard, city dwellers do not take adequate interest in the functioning of the urban government bodies. The multiplicity of special purpose agencies and other urban bodies confuses the public about their role boundaries.

How can We Empower Urban Local Governments?

Making Urban Local Bodies Financially Independent:

For the ULB to be independent and financially secure, fiscal decentralisation is very crucial.

Strengthening Municipal Revenue:

All Finance Commissions have recognized the need to augment property tax revenue to improve municipal finances. Especially: The 12th Finance Commission encouraged the use of the Geographical Information System (GIS) and digitization to improve property tax administration.

The 13th Finance Commission mandated the setting up of the State Property Tax Board as one of the conditions necessary for performance grant eligibility of states.

The aim of the State Property Tax Board is to help municipal corporations and municipal councils put in place a transparent and efficient property tax regime.

The 14th Finance Commission recommended that municipalities be enabled to levy vacant land tax.

Better Financial Database:

Lack of maintenance and audit of accounts at the local level leaves no verifiable financial data for municipalities leading to a denial of performance grants.

Both the 13th and the 14th Finance Commissions included better data availability as a conditionality for accessing performance grants.

Ensuring Active Citizen Participation:

For transparency and accountability in the governance process, there needs to be active citizen participation.

To ensure this, ULBs can create functional, decentralised platforms such as area sabhas and ward committees, which facilitate discussion and deliberation between elected representatives and citizens.

Creating Citizen Grievance Redressal Mechanism:

ULBs can establish a technology-enabled platform to register complaints, which will make city governments responsive to the needs of citizens.

Through this mechanism, citizens should also be allowed to provide feedback and close complaints.

Addressing these structural and architectural problems of urban governance will ensure effective service delivery in cities, improving the quality of life for its citizens.

Previous Year Questions (PYQ)

Q. Local self-government can be best explained as an exercise in (2017)

(a) Federalism

(b) Democratic decentralisation

(c) Administrative delegation

(d) Direct democracy

Ans: (b)

Q. The fundamental object of the Panchayati Raj system is to ensure which among the following? (2015)

People's participation in development

Political accountability

Democratic decentralisation

Financial mobilisation

Select the correct answer using the code given below

(a) 1, 2 and 3 only

(b) 2 and 4 only

(c) 1 and 3 only

(d) 1, 2, 3 and 4

Ans: (c)

CHAPTER THREE

Budget

The budget in its elementary form had been part of almost all monarchies of the history. There have been written documents regarding the existence of the state treasury, accountants and auditors who were employed by the monarchs to protect the royal treasury.

The modern democracies have the legislatures playing an important role in the managing of public finances. The taxes that are collected and the revenues that are generated by the government through several means are to be used for the development and welfare of the society. The emergence of the Welfare State made it important that the government money is being judiciously used to better the living conditions of society in general and the marginalized sections in particular.

The process of budgets fulfills important functions in the economy of the nation. They act as a means to carry out several objectives of the public organization. Some of the important roles of budget in the national economy are:

(i) Prioritization of the allocation of the public resources

(ii) Achieving policy goals through prudent financial planning

(iii) Establishing accountability regarding the usage of the tax payers money

(iv) Financial controls also ensure compliance to rules and increase in efficiency

In some countries, the executive part of the government also plays an important part regarding the revenues and expenditures of the government and the legislative is reduced to just an approving and reviewing authority, e.g. in UK where the budget process is primarily dominated by the executive (the House of Commons).

A more balanced approach of distributing power is practiced in the USA where the legislature can review and make changes to the budget presented by the President and the President finally approves it after satisfactory checks and balances are concluded.

The dominance of executive or legislature in the budgeting process is a matter of debate as many consider the legislative to be an obstacle in the fast paced globalized economy where foreign direct investment and monetary funding from organizations like IMF and World Bank is of crucial importance to several democracies. There are several measures suggested to expedite the decision making process from fixing the term of the legislatures, introducing citizen panels, attaching funding power at local levels to bringing in two year budgetary cycle and special legislation regarding expenditure management.

The government expenditure is funded by a common pool of tax payer's money and the policies that are formed with this money are further used to fund projects. The catch here lies in the fact that the people who actually are paying for these policies are the larger group while the people who benefit from these policies might be a much smaller group, which translates that one might not be enjoying the benefits for which one is paying money. Such scenario leads to an excessive spending of public money on policies which are not beneficial to the society as a whole. Such situations are prevalent in democracies which are multi-lingual, multi-ethnic and divided on the basis of regions, religions and other factors.

Merriam Webster defines Budget as a leather pouch, wallet or pack.

Oxford Dictionary defines budget as the money that is available to a person or an organization and a plan of how it will be spent over a period of time.

Types of Budgets in Public Administration

The public budgets are different from other forms of budgets in many ways; here the voters delegate the power of spending their money to the politicians or the elected representatives. Now having understood the concept of budget in the last article, let us understand the different kinds of budget that are there in the public financial management:

(i) Balanced Budget: As suggested by the name, a balanced budget is that which has no deficit or surplus. The revenues coming are equal to the expenditures.

(ii) Revenue Budget: It is just the details of the revenue received by the government through taxes and other sources and the expenditure that is met through it.

(iii) Performance Budget: This type of budget is mostly used by the organizations and ministries involved in the developmental activities. This process of budgeting takes into account the end result or the performance of the developmental program thus insuring cost effective and efficient planning. With the increasing developmental challenges and awareness regarding the usage of tax payer's money, new methods of budgeting are required of which the performance based budgeting has emerged as a transparent and accountable method.

It relies on three aspects of understanding of the final outcome, the strategies formulated to reach those final outcomes and the specific activities that were carried out to achieve those outcomes. With a very detailed and objective analysis, this budgeting process is very result oriented in its approach.

(iv) Zero based budget: Zero based budgeting has its clear advantage when the limited resources are to be allotted carefully and objectively. It is quite flexible in nature and relies on rational methods, systematic evaluation to reallocate resources and justify the usage of funds. It starts from a zero base unlike traditional budgets where incremental approach is used. Here, the needs and costs of every function of the organization are taken into consideration for the next year's budget. So the budget is futuristic and may or may not be equal or more from the last year's budget as traditionally calculated.

The budgets in the parliamentary kind of system similar to what exists in a country like India become a tool of political negotiations where the budgeting powers are delegated to the Finance Minister of the country.

In a single party government, the entire party shares the same views regarding the spending of the resources however; the disagreement arises when individual members may differ on the cost of the distributive policies and would want the government funds to be diverted to their respective electoral constituencies.

In a coalition government, the differing opinions are tackled through compromise and contracts approach where the coalition parties keeps the check on the budget process ensuring that it lies within the boundaries of the agreed contract. The infamous fallout between the ruling UPA and the Trinamool Congress over the Railway Budget last year is worth citing in reference to the current discussion.

In the presidential kind of system too, the executive plays a somewhat similar process. A significant change that happened in US regarding the budget process was the Budget Enforcement Act passed in 1990s under the Bush administration, which protected the budgetary parameters against later modifications once cleared in the budget summit between the president and the legislature.

The budget process in different systems of government may vary but they are all aligned to achieve the relevant economic and social goals of that country. With increasing globalization and interdependent economies, several external considerations also come into play when the budgets are designed. We shall learn about the budget process in the next section.

Budgetary Process in Different Countries

We have read earlier regarding the relevance of budget in the economies of the nations. Apart from the prioritization and allocation of resources and being an account of political compromises, victory and losses, budgets play one another important role. They are a mirror into the future; they create a picture of what the future consequences of current actions shall be, desirable or miserable. Budgets therefore have to be well thought out plans which should not aim at only short term benefits but also look at long term gains.

According to author Aaron B. Wildavsky, in the book, Budgeting: A comparative theory of budgeting processes, two very pertinent question which arises are:

(i) Who will plan the budgetary process, a central authority, decentralized or delegated authority or non-centralized independent authorities

(ii) How will the planning occur, through a central body which will form regulations or a price system acting through non-centralized units

The budgeting process has a lot to do with the available resources and wealth of a country. If the country is poor but the environmental conditions are stable and certain, the most commonly found budgeting method is revenue budgeting. When the wealth is absent i.e. a country is poor as well as the environment is uncertain, the budgeting process if that of repetitive budgeting. Repetitive budgeting is a common phenomenon for the poor countries where the budgeting happens several times over the year due to changing scenarios, limited funds and misplaced strategies.

The rich countries which have certain environments go for incremental budgeting and in case there are uncertainties, the incremental budget is alternated with repetitive budget. The difference in the budgeting process amongst different nations also happens because of their respective taxing system and the how and choice of programs they spend money on. So while, Japan has an electoral party, the Liberal Democratic Party which plays an important role in the budgeting process, France has a mixed Presedential-Parliamnetary system, the USA has an independent legislature and executive and the cabinet in UK is responsible for important decisions regarding revenues, taxes and expenditure.

In the USA, The Office of Management and Budget steer the President in realizing the budget goals. The respective government agencies put their request for funds which are reviewed. The House Appropriations Committee decides how much money should be given for each purpose however the final deciding power lies with the Congress. After the budget reforms of 1974, many sub committees gave up their guardianship and the role played by them was taken over by the higher House bodies.

In India, the Union Budget is presented by the Finance Minister every year in February. The process begins with a budget speech in the parliament which has two parts, one outlining the general economic scenario and the second part which contains details of the proposed taxations for the next financial year. A general discussion on the budget happens after few days of its presentation and a voting happens on the request for grants.

An important aspect of this process is the Cut Motions which allows the members of the upper house to question the policies and programs of the government where the money is being spent. These cut motions are of three types namely:

(i) Policy cut where the amount for demand is reduced by a meager Rs1 which also implies that the mover disapproves of the policy

(ii) Economic cut where the demand is reduced by a specific sum

(iii) Token cut is when the demand amount is reduced by Rs.100

The Parliamentary Committee plays a significant role only when the limited time of the parliament leads to the Guillotine situation where not all demands are discussed. In this situation, the department related standing committees and financial committees undertake the task to scrutinize in details, the government spending, expenditures and performance.

The budgetary process in UK is lengthy too, where the departments submit their funding requests or Main Supply Estimates to the HM or the Her Majesty's Treasury. The government then releases a consolidated document called the Central Government Supply Estimates for the year. Agencies have respective oversight committee in parliament which oversees the changes if any made in the requests submitted. The UK parliament does not take a decision upon the new budget until summer and therefore the funding for the respective agencies continue up until the new budget is enacted.

In the rapidly developing economy like China, the central agency that control budget is Ministry of Finance (MoF). The National Auditing Committee audits the MoF and the most common discrepancy cited by them was the over allocation than the budgeted amount or not allocating the sum mentioned in the budget requests. The Chinese legislature the National People's Congress lacks any substantial control over the budgeting process which is often cited as the root of the budgetary problems in China.

It would be interesting to learn more about the budget processes of other nations as well however, it lies beyond the scope of this particular article. However, it is recommended to the readers and students that they try to explore the budgetary process of nations like France and Germany and the contrasting countries like Somalia and Zimbabwe in Africa, Afghanistan as well as Pakistan, Bangladesh and Thailand in Asia.

Budgeting process in India

[The procedure for presentation of the Budget in and its passing by Lok Sabha is as laid down in articles 112—117 of the Constitution of India, Rules 204—221 and 331-E of the Rules of Procedure and Conduct of Business in Lok Sabha and Direction 19-B of Directions by the Speaker.]

Presentation of Budget

The Budget is presented to Lok Sabha in two parts, namely, the Railway Budget pertaining to Railway Finance and the General Budget which gives an overall picture of the financial position of the Government of India, excluding the Railways.

The Budget is presented to Lok Sabha on such day as the President may direct. Immediately after the presentation of the Budget, the following three statements under the Fiscal Responsibility and Budget Management Act, 2003 are also laid on the Table of Lok Sabha

(i) The Medium-Term Fiscal Policy Statement;

(ii) The Fiscal Policy Strategy Statement; and

(iii) The Macro Economic Framework Statement.

Simultaneously, a copy of the respective Budgets is laid on the Table of Rajya Sabha. In an election year, the Budgets may be presented twice—first to secure a Vote on Account for a few months and later in full.

Distribution of Budget Papers

In the case of the Railway Budget, the sets are distributed to members from the Publications Counter after the Railway Minister has concluded his speech. The sets of General Budget are distributed to members from several booths in the Inner and Outer Lobbies arranged according to the Division Numbers of members. In case Division Numbers have not been allotted, these booths are arranged State-wise. The budget papers are made available to members after the Finance Minister's speech is over, the Finance Bill has been introduced and the House has adjourned for the day.

Discussion on the Budget

No discussion on Budget takes place on the day it is presented to the House. Budgets are discussed in two stages—the General Discussion followed by detailed discussion and voting on the demands for grants.

Allotment of Time for Discussion

The whole process of discussion and voting on the demands for grants and the passage of the Appropriation and Finance Bills is to be completed within a specified time. As a result, often the demands for grants relating to all the Ministries/Departments cannot be discussed and demands of some Ministries get guillotined i.e. voted without discussion. The Minister of Parliamentary Affairs, after the presentation of the Budget, holds a meeting of leaders of Parties/Groups in Lok Sabha for the selection of Ministries/Departments whose demands for grants might be discussed in the House. On the basis of decisions arrived at this meeting, the Government forwards the proposals for the consideration of the Business Advisory Committee. The Business Advisory Committee after considering the proposals allots time and also recommends the order in which the demands might be discussed. It is generally left to the Government to make any change in the order of discussion.

After the allotment of time by the Business Advisory Committee, a time table showing the dates on and order in which the demands for grants of various Ministries would be taken up in the House is published in Bulletin-Part II for the information of members.

General Discussion on the Budget

During the General Discussion, the House is at liberty to discuss the Budget as a whole or any question of principles involved therein but no motion can be moved. A general survey of administration is in order. The scope of discussion is confined to an examination of the general scheme and structure of the Budget, whether the items of expenditure ought to be increased or decreased, the policy of taxation as expressed in the Budget and in the speech of the Finance Minister. The Finance Minister or the Railway Minister, as the case may be, has the general right of reply at the end of the discussion.

Consideration of the Demands for Grants by Departmentally Related Standing Committees of Parliament

With the creation of Departmentally Related Standing Committees of Parliament in 1993, the Demands for Grants of all the Ministries/Departments are required to be considered by these Committees. After the General Discussion on the Budget is over, the House is adjourned for a fixed period. During this period, the Demands for Grants of the Ministries/Departments are considered by the Committees. These Committees are required to make their reports to the House within specified period without asking for more time and make separate report on the Demands for Grants of each Ministry.

Discussion on Demands for Grants

The demands for grants are presented to Lok Sabha along with the Annual Financial Statement. These are not generally moved in the House by the Minister concerned. The demands are assumed to have been moved and are proposed from the Chair to save the time of the House. After the reports of the Standing Committees are presented to the House, the House proceeds to the discussion and voting on Demands for Grants, Ministry-wise. The scope of discussion at this stage is confined to a matter which is under the administrative control of the Ministry and to each head of the demand as is put to the vote of the House. It is open to members to disapprove a policy pursued by a particular Ministry or to suggest measure for economy in the administration of that Ministry or to focus attention of the Ministry to specific local grievances. At this stage, cut motions can be moved to reduce any demand for grant but no amendments to a motion seeking to reduce any demand is permissible.

Cut Motions

The motions to reduce the amounts of demands for grants are called 'Cut Motions'. The object of a cut motion is to draw the attention of the House to the matter specified therein.

Cut Motions can be classified into three categories:—
(i) Disapproval of Policy Cut;
(ii) Economy Cut ; and
(iii) Token Cut.

Disapproval of Policy Cut: A cut motion which says "That the amount of the demand be reduced to Re. 1" implies that the mover disapproves of the policy underlying the demand. The member giving notice of such a Cut Motion has to indicate in precise terms the particulars of the policy which he proposes to discuss. Discussion is confined to the specific point or points mentioned in the notice and it is open to the member to advocate an alternative policy.

Economy Cut: Where the object of the motion is to effect economy in the expenditure, the form of the motion is "That the amount of the demand be reduced by Rs...(a specified amount)". The amount suggested for reduction may be either a lump-sum reduction in the demand or omission or reduction of an item in the demand.

Token Cut: Where the object of the motion is to ventilate a specific grievance within the sphere of responsibility of the Government of India, its form is: "That the amount of the demand be reduced by Rs. 100". Discussion on such a cut motion is confined to the particular grievance specified in the motion which is within the sphere of responsibility of the Government of India.

For the facility of members, printed forms for giving notices of cut motions are kept in the Parliamentary Notice Office.

Role of Budget

The efficiency and effectiveness of the operation of any public or private enterprise depends on the control available to management in almost every organization. Therefore the number of activities going on must be recorded for attainment of the organization goals.

The role of budget and budgetary control has become a very vital financial control and accountability device in the public sector and provide a formal basis for monitoring the progress of the entire economy. The organization must economize resources and discover the means of achieving a specific plan.

The Institution of Cost and Management Accounting (CIMA) defined budget as a financial or quantitative statement prepared and approved prior to defined period of time of the policy to be pursed during the period for the purpose of attaining a given objectives. It may include income, expenditure and the employment capital.

Often than not when these plans are put into operation, conditions prevail which tends to cause deviation from the plan and corrective measures are always taken to steer the organization back on the right track.

On the other hand, budgetary control is the establishment of policies and the periodic preview or comparison of the actual result with the budgeted performance either to secure approval for individual actions or serve as a remedial course of action.

Budget and budgetary control deals with the issue of making good potential plan based on the revenues, expenditure, assets, liabilities and cash flow for a defined period of time which is necessary in governmental unit at every level to make financial plan in order to carry out routine operations which will help in making financial decision.

Significance and Concept of Budget in Public Administration

The budget in its elementary form had been part of almost all monarchies of the history. There have been written documents regarding the existence of the state treasury, accountants and auditors who were employed by the monarchs to protect the royal treasury.

The modern democracies have the legislatures playing an important role in the managing of public finances. The taxes that are collected and the revenues that are generated by the government through several means are to be used for the development and welfare of the society. The emergence of the Welfare State made it important that the government money is being judiciously used to better the living conditions of society in general and the marginalized sections in particular.

The process of budgets fulfills important functions in the economy of the nation. They act as a means to carry out several objectives of the public organization.

Some of the important roles of budget in the national economy are:

Prioritization of the allocation of the public resources.

Achieving policy goals through prudent financial planning.

Establishing accountability regarding the usage of the tax payers money.

Financial controls also ensure compliance to rules and increase in efficiency.

In some countries, the executive part of the government also plays an important part regarding the revenues and expenditures of the government and the legislative is reduced to just an approving and reviewing authority, e.g. in UK where the budget process is primarily dominated by the executive (the House of Commons).

A more balanced approach of distributing power is practiced in the USA where the legislature can review and make changes to the budget presented by the President and the President finally approves it after satisfactory checks and balances are concluded.

The dominance of executive or legislature in the budgeting process is a matter of debate as many consider the legislative to be an obstacle in the fast paced globalized economy where foreign direct investment and monetary funding from organizations like IMF and World Bank is of crucial importance to several democracies. There are several measures suggested to expedite the decision making process from fixing the term of the legislatures, introducing citizen panels, attaching funding power at local levels to bringing in two year budgetary cycle and special legislation regarding expenditure management.

The government expenditure is funded by a common pool of tax payer's money and the policies that are formed with this money are further used to fund projects. The catch here lies in the fact that the people who actually are paying for these policies are the larger group while the people who benefit from these policies might be a much smaller group, which translates that one might not be enjoying the benefits for which one is paying money. Such scenario leads to an excessive spending of public money on policies which are not beneficial to the society as a whole. Such situations are prevalent in democracies which are multi-lingual, multi-ethnic and divided on the basis of regions, religions and other factors.

Indian Budget : A Brief History

The budget is announced to disclose agenda regarding government's future expenditure to strengthen nation's economy and consolidate economic stability through tax proposals.

India has had 25 finance ministers since Independence in 1947.

The word budget is derived from bowgette, which means 'a leather bag' in French. The budget is announced to disclose the government's future expenditures intended to strengthen the nation's economy and consolidate economic stability through tax proposals.

The budget was first introduced in India on 7 April 1860 by the East-India Company to the British Crown. Pre-independence finance minister, James Wilson presented the budget in 1860.

One week prior to the disclosure, publishers of the budget under the finance ministry are kept isolated from the press and other sources.

Earlier budget papers were printed in Rashtrapati Bhavan. The printing venue was shifted to Minto Road in New Delhi. Since 1980, budget papers are printed in the North Block.

Shanmukham Chetty, first Finance Minister of India presented the budget in November 1947 without any tax proposals. However , he presented the analysis of the economic scenario of Independent India just 95 days before the budget presentation in 1948.

Liaquat Ali Khan was the finance minister of the All India Muslim League from October 1946 to Independence in 1947.

After Chetty, K.C Neogy took charge of the finance department for 35 days. John Mathai was the third finance minister to present the budget in 1950-51 before C.D. Deshmukh, who presented the budget in the newly formed Indian Parliament. Deshmukh was the first Indian RBI governor and Finance Minister from 1950 to 1956.

Budget papers in Hindi were being printed from 1955 onwards.

Jawaharlal Nehru, the first Prime Minister presented the budget when he was Union Finance Minister as well in 1958-1959. Later in 1959, Morarji Desai when became Finance Minister, he presented the budget 10 times, a record so far. He presented two budgets on February 29 on his birthday in the years 1964 and 1968.

The budget of 1973-74 is known as the 'Black Budget' as the nation had a deficit of Rs. 550 crore.

After Desai's resignation in 1979, Indira Gandhi took over as the first and only female Finance Minister of India.

The 1987 budget was presented by Rajiv Gandhi after V.P. Singh quit the government. Gandhi introduced the corporate tax.

In 1991, Yashwant Sinha from NDA presented the interim budget, but in the same year Congress regained its power and appointed Manmohan Singh as Finance Minister. In 1991, he introduced the concept of service tax and foreign investment proposals and reduction of peak import duty from 300 percent to 50 percent.

P. Chidambaram in 1996 presented the budget without a debate, following constitutional crises during I.K. Gujral's prime-ministership. A year later, he again proposed the 'Dream Budget'.

Till the year 2000, the Union Budget was announced at 5 PM, but Yashwant Sinha began a new trend by announcing it at 11 AM in 2001.

The 'Sarva Siksha Abhiyan Programme' was announced during the 2001 budget when Atal Bihari Vajpayee was the prime minister.

Yashwant Sinha's 1991, 1999, 2000 and 2001 budgets followed Forex crises, the Pokhran blasts, the Kargil war and Gujarat earthquake respectively.

The National Rural Health Mission, Gender Budget and NREGA schemes were announced in the 2005-06 budget.

Morarji Desai topped the list with 10 budget presentations. Pranab Mukherjee, P Chidambaram, Yashwant Sinha, Y B Chavan and C D Deshmukh are next with seven budget presentations each.

Manmohan Singh and T T Krishnamachari presented six budgets each and R Venkatraman and H M Patel presented three budgets as Finance Minister.

Jaswant Singh, V P Singh, C Subramaniam, John Mathai and R K Shanmukham got an opportunity to present budgets twice.

Budget system in pre-colonial period
Extracts From The Arthashastra: A Mauryan Budget

In the Mauryan 'budget', the budget and accounts were to be prepared annually, with the year being of 354 days.

One of the most important events of the annual financial calendar in India is the presentation of the union budget in the Indian parliament, a thoroughly modern attribute of the running of a modern nation state. In actual fact a 'budget', leather bag of the 15th century which became a set of fiscal plans in the 18th century, in whatever form or rubric, is essential to the running of any country at any time. And so it was for the period of the Mauryans.

The Arthashastra of Kautilya sets down a well-defined structure for the financial ordering of a kingdom. It is a theoretical treatise and cannot be taken as a manual of the financial ordering of the Mauryan state. When studied together with evidence from other sources, Greek, Buddhist, Jain and also the inscriptions of Samrat Ashok, however, it appears that Mauryan budgeting could have approximated to the theoretical structure set up in book two of this ancient compendium on politics and economics.

The budget and accounts were to be prepared annually, with the year being of 354 days. Entries were made with reference to the king's regnal year, 'rajavarsham' which was made to coincide with the work year, ending on the full moon day of the month of Ashadha (June/July); what we today recognise as the day of Guru Poornima. Individual date entries were made as per year, month, fortnight and day.

The 'Samaharta' or the mantri whom we would call the Finance Minister today, was responsible for the preparation of the budget and accounts. He was to fix the amount of revenue to be collected from all the heads of income and then to arrange the income under the aayamukhas or sources. He was enjoined to show an increase in revenue and a reduction in expenditure and to try and address the problem of excess of expenditure over income if this should arise.

To explain further:

The items of revenue were called the 'aayasharira' or the body of income and classified under seven heads, city, country, mines, irrigation works, forests, cattle herds and trade routes.

The incomes from the city consisted of customs duties, fines, income from weights and measures department, issue of passports, liquor, yarn, ghee, goldsmiths, prostitutes, gambling, artists, temples etc. Quite a varied collection of income sources, some which would be frowned upon now! From the country came income from agriculture; salt, minerals and precious stones provided income from mines.

The irrigation-works head collected income from flowers, fruits vegetable sales, etc. and forests and cattle herds collected what we would now call income from animal husbandry. Given the pivotal importance of trade for the Mauryan empire, trade routes were a separate and important head of their own. The revenue from these heads was further classified into seven 'aayamukhas' or sources- price, share, tax, duty, levy, surcharge or penalty.

On the expenditure side or the 'vyayasharira' there were fifteen heads, including firstly, expenditure for worship of the gods and charity.

The most important heads were those related to the armed forces, the armoury and the palace. Stores, factories, labourers, maintenance of animal wealth were other important heads of expenditure. Majority of the expenditure was on state account and only a few can be construed as part of the king's privy purse (salaries for all the royals except the king were also fixed at a specific level).

Expenditure heads do not detail any items spent on state enterprises such as mining probably because the revenue is net income after deducting expenses.

The same principle applies to all items of revenue. Revenue estimate, accrued revenue, outstanding revenue, income, expenditure and balance were the accounting concepts used to try and present an accurate picture of the kingdom's budgetary situation at the end of the year going forward into the next one. All these are precisely defined in the Arthashastra and it would be an interesting exercise to compare them with accounting standards today.

A budget estimate of the revenue was made at the beginning of the year with refernce to different areas of economic activity and administrative units such as the village, district, region, etc. The Samaharta (or his office) fixed these estimates and they had to be strictly adhered to by the officers responsible for rendering this revenue to the state stores.

Incomes were classified as current, outstanding and derived from other sources; daily revenue was 'current', that belonging to the preceding year or transferred from another sphere of activity was 'outstanding' and fines, compensation, take-over of property, treasure, increase in prices etc. was 'income from other source's.

Expenditure was also classified into four types, day to day, after fixed intervals of time and unforeseen expenditure arising under these two heads classified separately. After the calculation of revenue and the deduction of expenditure from it, what remained was the balance which was received and carried forward.

One should also keep in mind that most of the revenue received by the state was in kind and there was a complex establishment of state stores headed by the 'Sannidhatri'.

Another office of great significance concerning the budget was the 'Akshapataladhyaksha' or the head of the records-cum-audit office, what we now know as the Comptroller and Auditor General. This establishment was completely separate from the Samaharta and the records maintained by it were to check the accounts kept by the Samaharta's office.

A comparison with heads in the annual financial statement of the union budget for 2017 will be interesting. The receipts into the Consolidated Fund of India are from tax sources, including income tax, corporation tax and indirect taxes and non-tax sources including fiscal services, interest dividends and profits.

Expenditure is on general services, social services and economic services. General services include the expenditure on keeping the state up and running i.e. expenses on the legislature, executive, judiciary apart from tax administration and defence. Economic services heads include areas such as disbursements on animal husbandry, irrigation, mines and minerals, industries, rural development and transport and communication.

A quick look shows the parallels-tax resources on the revenue side and similar disbursement heads on the expenditure side.

An interesting difference between Kautilyan and modern budgeting, however, is the lack of specific differentiation on capital and revenue account in the former although Kautilya is by no means ignorant of the differences in the impact and implications of the two and we do get hints of the results of different types of spending.

The provisions for budgeting and accounting in the Arthashastra and its resonance with modern budgeting has led some scholars to posit economic planning by the Kautilyan or Mauryan state, but this needs further study. For one, modern budgeting has a significant developmental push and economic planning is to that end, which is not so in the Mauryan budget.

In the words of R P Kangle, the emphasis in modern planning and budgeting is on development but that in the Arthashastra accounting methods is on control.

The complex machinery of accounting and auditing was set up so that the fruits of economic activity accrue without fail, to the State. The modern 'development' mantra, for all its failings is the major thrust of budgets today but we do not, of course, hear of it explicitly in the Kautilyan budget. This is in keeping with the Kautilyan focus on getting resources so that the King can spend them on the 'palana' or administration of his subjects.

Which of the two led to greater prosperity for the people at large is an open question until a comparative economic study of relative prosperity in ancient and modern India is conducted.

After two decades in the Indian Revenue Service Sumedha Verma Ojha now follows her passion, Ancient India; writing and speaking across the world on ancient Indian history, society, women, religion and the epics. Her Mauryan series is 'Urnabhih'; a Valmiki Ramayan in English and a book on the 'modern' women of ancient India.

Budget system in colonial period

Etymologically, the term budget is related to Latin bulga, which refers to a 'leather bag.' The term comes from a Gaulish source connected to the Irish bolg, which means a bag. It got associated with finance in mid 18th century following up a pamphlet titled "The Budget Opened" sarcastically attacking the tax plans of Great Britain's first Prime Minister Sir Robert Walpole. However, the term budget was first used in 1760 for statement of the actual results of receipts and expenditure in the preceding fiscal year presented in House of Commons by UK's Chancellor of Exchequer. The term budget was used in current context only after mid 19th century. 20th century was a stimulating era for budgeting. It was only after 1950s that budget was more rationally used for public planning and policy. The development of the theoretical framework of budgeting during 20th century has been shaped by the political, social and administrative players and circumstances.

During the 20th century, while the Budget and Accounting Act 1921 systematized the budgeting in USA, the Parliament Act 1911 excluded the Lords in UK to refuse money bills, thus depriving House of Lords of its power of veto over financial legislation. Since then, the elected House of Commons has supreme powers regarding budget decisions in UK and same was followed in India where Lok Sabha has such powers.

Key Points: Evolution of Indian Budget

A rough budget of East India Company was prepared in 1790. After the end of East India's Company's rule, India's first budget was presented on February 18, 1860 by James Wilson, a Finance Member of the India Council. The Finance Member's work was to advise the Viceroy on financial matters.

After the Morley-Minto Reforms of 1909, the Finance Member had to present his estimates to the Central Legislature in first quarter of every year. The Finance Member's presentation was followed by discussions on Budget proposals. During discussions, the members of the legislature could propose alterations in tax provisions, loans and grants to local government. The Finance Member was able to accept or reject these proposals but he needed to justify why he accepted some proposals and why rejected others.

Initially, the Railway budget was part of the general budget. On the basis of recommendations Acworth Committee, the Rail Budget was separated in 1924. That system follows till date. Recently, the Bibek Debroy committee has recommended to abolish the separate Railway Budget in a period of five years. The first budget of Independent and united India was presented by John Mathai in 1949-50. This budget also included the financial statements for former Princely States. The decision of forming a planning commission was declared in this budget.

The Four Stages of The Budget Process

Before we even think of answering the question and making our topic for discussion today it is very important that we start by defining the term budget. Most people use this term but do not really have a clear understanding of what it means. A budget is an estimate of the income and expenditure of an entity. This is over a given period of time and prepared through four stages of the Budget Process. Luckily this article covers the Key Four Stages of The Budget Process. These are budget preparation, budget authorization, budget execution and accountability which the USA, Canada and the UK have adopted as budget-making process guides since the 1960s as part of the 4 steps of the budgeting process.

This gives a guideline of how the entity's resources will be distributed in order to achieve organizational goals without going off-budget. In short, a budget serves as a guide to how much you need to spend for what reason. Usually, budgets are designed according to the available resources.

We hear a lot about government budgets. However, very few know the process by which this budget matures to a stage where it can be dished out to the public. The process we speak of is four stages of the Budget process which not only works for governments but also applies to small businesses that use budgets as the basis of their operations.

No stage is to be overlooked and a systematic way of carrying them out one by one needs to be formulated taking into consideration your business' expenses and whether or not they have a positive effect on your profitability.

The Four Stages Of The Budget Process

The 4 steps of the budgeting process include budget preparation, budget authorization, budget execution and accountability. Let us take a look at the four stages of the budget process/cycle in detail as explained below!

Preparation and Submission

The structure begins with a thought and a budget is in itself a structure that needs to be created. From this standpoint, the thought process precedes the creation of a budget. You need to consider factors like how much income is needed and, if the available resources permit, what new initiatives can be included.

Let's take for instance a small business owner whose creations and growth/development plans for the company determine what sails through the budget during these four stages of the budget process.

In the case of bigger corporations or even governments, budgets are prepared by finance units in their jurisdiction. Then, they are submitted to the powers that be. This process leads us to the next stage of the budget process as everything is now in their hands.

Approval

The atmosphere at this stage in the political sphere is quite different from that of the corporate world. In the latter, the company owner can simply stamp his signature in approval or not out of his discretion and maybe after a few consultations. Whereas in political circles, yes or no is not enough. Instead debates around the budget are held before approval.

Because of political differences among the leaders, the political process can negatively impact issues of priority. If businesses with larger boards fall victim to this bug, bankruptcy is imminent on the 4 steps of the budgeting process. A piece of advice to small business owners, like myself, who handle all four stages of the budget cycle themselves; it is important that your accountant (if you have one) or trusted colleague goes through your budget before you stamp it.

Execution

Of course, when approved, a budget has to be implemented. That is what is meant by the term 'execution.' Governments tend to focus more on reducing spending and they put tight bottlenecks around funds. This doesn't have to be the case in your business. You just have to devise a means of regulating expenditure and managing lower-than-expected revenue.

In my research, I came across this quote and I felt it is indeed profound to share four stages of the budget process; "Most of the time money comes in and goes out in accordance with the budget. A good budget isn't a limitation on what your company can spend. It's a financial embodiment of your company's strategy and tactics for the year."

Evaluation and Audit.

This is one of the most important stages of the budget cycle. Evaluation is an important aspect of all aspects of the business. It is not limited to budgets or finance. Some call this a progress check. No matter how good your budget is in concept, you have to frequently evaluate it and sometimes do revisions. Businesses have external stakeholders that can influence your business such that changes are inevitable. Customers and partner companies are some of these stakeholders.

Sometimes evaluation then reveals the flaws of some ideas you thought were so perfect. It also feeds into audits that trace how funds are used, dollar for dollar.

According to an observation, "The government audits and evaluates spending to ensure that money is being spent lawfully. But ongoing evaluation of your business' budget requires a wider lens of these Four stages of the budget process. You'll want to keep an eye on how effectively money is being spent. But what really matters in business is whether you're operating at a profit after mastering what are the four stages of the budget process."

Now we understand the four stages of the budget process which we now know as the budget cycle. My hope is we use this advice obtained as we journeyed through this article on the four stages of the Budget process. I prefer the word 'cycle' to 'process' more.

The former clearly shows us that this is not a once and for all process. In fact, the budget document is a living one from which amendments, additions and subtractions draw hybrids of budgets. It would be very useful if we use diagrams and graphs clearly show the four stages of the Budget process. These are really useful as they show us exactly how your income, expenditure and revenue are performing and what are the four stages of the budget process".

We also need to pay attention to the budget protocols by governments in order for us to understand our own businesses and the capacities they can hold under our respective governments.

Types of Central Government Funds - Indian Polity

There are three types of funds of the Central Government – Consolidated Fund of India (Article 266), Contingency Fund of India (Article 267) and Public Accounts of India (Article 266) mentioned in the Indian Constitution.

Funds of Government of India

The Indian government's funds are kept in three parts, which are listed below:
Consolidated Fund of India
Contingency Fund of India
Public Accounts of India
All three are described below briefly.

Consolidated Fund of India

This is the most important of all accounts of the government.
This fund is filled by:
Direct and indirect taxes
Loans taken by the Indian government
Returning of loans/interests of loans to the government by anyone/agency that has taken it
The government meets all its expenditure from this fund.
The government needs parliamentary approval to withdraw money from this fund.
The provision for this fund is given in Article 266(1) of the Constitution of India.
Each state can have its own Consolidated Fund of the state with similar provisions.
The Comptroller and Auditor General of India audits these funds and reports to the relevant legislatures on their management.

Contingency Fund of India

Provision for this fund is made in Article 267(1) of the Constitution of India.
Its corpus is Rs. 500 crores. It is in the nature of an imprest (money maintained for a specific purpose).
The Secretary of Finance Ministry holds this fund on behalf of the President of India.
This fund is used to meet unexpected or unforeseen expenditure.
Each state can have its own contingency fund established under Article 267(2)

Public Accounts of India

This is constituted under Article 266(2) of the Constitution.

All other public money (other than those covered under the Consolidated Fund of India) received by or on behalf of the Indian Government are credited to this account/fund.

This is made up of:

Bank savings account of the various ministries/departments

National small savings fund, defense fund

National Investment Fund (money earned from disinvestment)

National Calamity & Contingency Fund (NCCF) (for Disaster Management)

Provident fund, Postal insurance, etc.

Similar funds

The government does not need permission to take advances from this account.

Each state can have its own similar accounts.

The audit of all the expenditure from the Public Account of India is taken up by the CAG.

Controller General of Accounts (CGA)

The CGA is the Principal Accounting Adviser to the Government of India. The office is in the Department of Expenditure, Ministry of Finance, GOI.

CGA is responsible for establishing and maintaining a technically sound Management Accounting System.

It also prepares and submits the accounts of the Central Government.

It is also in charge of the exchequer control and internal audits.

Types of Expenditures

Charged Expenditures

Non-votable charges are called charged expenditures.

No voting takes place for this amount which is spent from the Consolidated Fund of India. Parliamentary approval is not needed.

These are paid whether or not the budget is passed.

Emoluments, allowances and expenditure of the President and his office, salary and allowances of chairman, Deputy chairman of Rajya Sabha, Speaker, Supreme Court judges, CAG and Deputy Speaker of the Lok Sabha come under this expenditure.

Another example of charged expenditure is debt charges of the government.

These are not voted because these payments are deemed guaranteed by the state.

Even though voting does not take place, discussion on these can take place in both the Houses.

Expenses Charged on Consolidated Fund of India

The following expenses are charged on the Consolidated fund of India:

President's Emoluments and allowances and other expenditure relating to his office

Chairman and the Deputy Chairman of the Rajya Sabha and the Speaker and the Deputy Speaker of the Lok Sabha – Salaries and allowances

Salaries, allowances and pensions of the Supreme Court's judges

Pensions of the High Courts' judges

Comptroller and Auditor General of India's salaries, allowances and pensions

Salaries, allowances and pension of the chairman and members of the Union Public Service Commission

Administrative expenses of the Supreme Court, the office of the Comptroller and Auditor General of India and the Union Public Service Commission including the salaries, allowances and pensions of the persons serving in these offices

The debt charges for which the Government of India is liable, including interest, sinking fund charges and redemption charges and other expenditure relating to the raising of loans and the service and redemption of debt

Any sum required to satisfy any judgement, decree or award of any court or arbitral tribunal

Any other expenditure declared by the Parliament to be so charged

Voted/Votable Expenditures

This is the actual budget.

The expenditures in the budget are actually in the form of Demand for Grants.

The demands for grants are presented to the Lok Sabha along with the Annual Financial Statement. Generally, one Demand for Grant is presented for each Ministry or Department.

Supplementary Grants

Supplementary grants are granted when the sum approved by the Parliament via the appropriation act for a certain service for the current financial year is found to be inadequate.

Additional Grants

These are granted when a need has emerged for the duration of the present financial year for additional expenditure for certain new service, not considered in the budget for that year.

Excess Grants

Excess Grant is granted when the cash spent on any provision in a financial year exceeds the amount granted for that service in the budget.

Questions related to Types of Funds of Govt. of India

Who controls government money in India?

The Ministry of Finance is the apex controlling authority.

Who holds the Contingency Fund of India?

The Secretary to the Government of India, Ministry of Finance, Department of Economic Affairs holds the Fund on behalf of the President of India.

Who gets salary from Consolidated Fund of India?

Salary and Allowances of the President, Speaker/Deputy Speaker of Lok Sabha, Chairman/Deputy Chairman of Rajya Sabha, Salaries and Allowances of Supreme Court judges, Pensions of Supreme Court as well as High Court Judges, Salaries and Allowances of CAG, Lok Pal.

Who prepares the budget in India?

The Ministry of Finance prepares the budget.

Budgeting Cycle – Meaning, Importance, Phases and More

Budgeting Cycle or budget cycle refers to the steps or phases that a company or an individual, or a government organization needs to go through to come up with a budget. The budget is the estimation of the expenses that a company expects to incur in the future.

We can also say that the budget cycle is the life of the budget, starting from developing a budget to assessing it. Often businesses that make the budget go through these phases without even realizing they are following the budget cycle.

Budgeting Cycle – Importance

The budgeting cycle is mainly of use to the government agencies, which need to come up with a transparent budgeting process. However, nowadays, businesses are also readily using the concept and customizing it as per their needs. Generally, a budget cycle is longer than the company's accounting period. It starts before the accounting period and ends after the accounting period.

Following the budget cycle makes the whole process intelligent and accountable. It is because the entire process uses research, past data, and estimates. Also, since the segments of the budget cycle are well defined, it encourages the budget creator to meet all the guidelines, such as constant input and revision, to come up with an accurate budget.

Thus, we can say that the budget cycle helps to control costs, assist the finance department in the preparation of the reports, and help management make more informed decisions.

Now that you know the importance of a budget cycle, let's talk about phases in the budgeting cycle.

Stages/Phases

The budgeting cycle primarily involves four phases – preparing and submitting, approving, executing, and monitoring.

Preparing and Submitting Budget

The first phase in the budgeting cycle is to create the budget. A business must use its leadership vision to decide on what to include and exclude from the budget. Also, the management should take the suggestions and recommendations of the ground-level employees. A budget must include targeted revenue and the estimates of expenses that a business needs to incur to meet the revenue targets. Also, the budget should consist of any improvements that a company expects to go for in the near term.

Once the budget is ready, it needs to be approved by the department heads and the top management.

Getting the Budget Approved

Approving the budget is not just a simple yes or no. Instead, it may involve extensive debates before a budget gets final approval. A budget may move back and forth for edits and corrections until all parties approve the document.

If possible, the business must extensively discuss the budget involving all the stakeholders. In the case of a small company or sole proprietorship, the owner must discuss the budget with the accountant or have an independent authority to review it. The budget should get approval only after the review, discussion, edit, and corrections (if any).

Executing the Budget

Once you get the approval for the budget, the next step is to start executing it. The execution of the budget usually starts with the beginning of the accounting period. Generally, the business operations are performed following the budget. If the revenues and expenses are not as per the budget, then you should use your business tactics to manage the situation. However, you should not let the budget impede or limit your business decisions.

A business must create and maintain spending records. Such records help in ensuring internal and external accountability. They also serve as useful data points for the next budget cycle. Such records also help to identify trouble spots or opportunities to save some funds or earn more revenues.

Evaluating/ Monitoring The Budget

A company or an individual should regularly evaluate the budget. Regular evaluation helps make timely revisions to the budget based on internal and external factors. These changes could be revising revenue targets, adjusting costs, or making an adjustment to the budget with any newly available information.

Regular evaluation is also necessary to identify variance, if any. Variation is the deviation of the actual spending from budget spending. Even when evaluating the budget, the focus should be on boosting the profits.

A final evaluation of the budget is done after the end of the accounting period. This evaluation provides the overall feedback on the budget, including how accurate it was, cash flow management, and more. Such feedback helps in the preparation of the next budget and assists management in making better financial decisions.

Budget Cycle vs. Budget Period

As said above, the budget cycle is usually longer than the accounting period. A budget cycle includes the time for planning, preparing, approving, executing, and evaluating the budget. The budget period, on the other hand, is the actual period to which the budget applies.

For example, if a company prepares the budget quarterly, then the budget period will be three months. But the budget cycle will start before the quarter and end after the quarter completes.

Types of Budget Cycle

A budget cycle is primarily monthly, quarterly, and annually.

Monthly Budget Cycle

The budget period starts on the first day and ends on the last day of the month. Since different months have a different number of days, the monthly total will differ from month to month. A business usually maintains twelve budget cycles in a monthly budget cycle, but these are mostly at the department level. Also, the monthly budget cycle covers only a few income and expense items.

Quarterly Budget Cycle

These are more popular than the monthly budget cycles. It is because they reduce the burden on the company in terms of preparing, monitoring, and analyzing the budget. Also, quarterly budgets are more useful if the business of the company is seasonal.

Annual Budget Cycle

It is the most current budget cycle. The annual budget period for most companies globally is from January 1 to December 31.

Final Words

As the word budget cycle suggests, budgeting is an ongoing process. Once a company is done with one budget cycle, it gets time to start preparing for the next budget cycle. And, the business, or individual or the government, would go through the above phases all over again. There is an exclusive department for big companies that deal with budgeting and always remain busy with budget cycle activity.

Enactments of Budget in the Parliament

It is also called as 'enactments of budget' which means converting the two bills into acts. The passage in Parliament has five stages:

(1) Presentation of budget,

(2) General discussion,

(3) Voting on demands for grants,

(4) Passing of Appropriation Bill,

(5) Passing of Finance Bill.

Article 112 of the Constitution enjoins upon the President of India to get the budget presented before both of the houses of Parliament. Being a Money Bill, it has to be presented to the Lok Sabha first and must classify the charge on the Consolidated Fund and expenditure on the Consolidated Fund of India separately.

There is a prescribed legislative procedure in each house and the Rajya Sabha should not delay it for more than fourteen days. The Consolidated Fund, Contingency Fund and public account transactions are updated to appraise the Parliament which operates the Consolidated Fund at the President's disposal and takes stock of public account assets and liabilities without voting on them. The budget in India had to pass through three readings without any committee stage.

The first reading is called the presentation of the budget which includes the following documents:

(1) The economic survey report,

(2) Economic classification of the budget,

(3) Annual reports of the ministries,

(4) An explanatory memorandum on the budget,

(5) An Appropriation Bill and

(6) A Finance Bill containing the taxation proposals.

The presentation of the budget to the Lok Sabha is in two or more parts and each part ends within the manner as if it were the budget. Accordingly, the budget is presented as Railway Budget and as General Budget. The introduction of Railway Budget precedes that of the General Budget.

While the former is presented to the Lok Sabha by the railway minister in the third week of February, the latter is presented to the Lok Sabha by the finance minister on the last working day of February. The finance minister presents the General Budget with a speech known as the 'budget speech'. At the end of the budget speech in the Lok Sabha, the budget is laid before the Rajya Sabha which can only discuss it and has no power to vote on the demand for grants.

The general discussion on budget takes place during budget session. It lasts for three to four days. During this stage, the Lok Sabha can discuss the budget as a whole or on any question of principle involved therein but no motion is moved or submitted for the vote of the House. The finance minister has a right of reply at the end of the discussion. After the general discussion on budget, the Lok Sabha takes up voting of demands for grants.

They are presented ministry-wise and a demand becomes a grant after it has been voted. The voting of demands for grants is the exclusive privilege of the Lok Sabha and not of Rajya Sabha. The voting is confined to the votable part of the budget but the expenditure charged on the Consolidated Fund of India can only be discussed.

The General Budget has totally 109 demands (103 for civil expenditure and 6 for defence expenditure), the Railway Budget has 32 demands. Each demand is voted separately by the Lok Sabha. During this stage, the members of Parliament can discuss the details of the budget. They can also move to reduce any demand for grant. But increase or upward revisions of estimates are not permissible.

The members who propose reduction of grant bring three kinds of cut motions which are either withdrawn or dropped because their passing will be tantamount to a vote of no confidence in the government. Still to attract the attention of the government, the cut motions are moved to bring a moral pressure on the executive.

These cut motions are:

(1) Token Cut Motion: It expresses a specific grievance which is within the sphere of responsibility of the government. It states that the amount of the demand be reduced by Rs 100. On the 26th day, the Speaker puts all the remaining demands to vote and disposes them whether they have been discussed by the members or not. This is called as 'Guillotine closer'.

(2) Policy Cut Motion shows disapproval of the policy underlying a demand. It states that the amount of the demand be reduced to Re 1.

(3) Economy Cut Motion asks for economy in the proposed expenditure. It states that the amount of the demand be reduced by a specified amount which may be either a lump sum reduction or omission or reduction of an item in the demand.

Article 113 and 114 provide for the presentation of various kinds of demands for grants by the Parliament. Some of them are:

(1) Vote on credit
(2) Vote on accounts
(3) Vote on exceptional grants
(4) Supplementary grants
(5) Excess grants
(6) Token grants

In addition to the budget, various other kinds of grants are made by the Parliament under extraordinary or special circumstances. When the amount authorized by the Parliament through the Appropriation Act for a particular service for the current financial year is found to be insufficient for the purposes of that year supplementary grants are sanctioned by the Parliament.

Similarly, when a need has arisen during the current financial year for additional expenditure upon some new service not contemplated in the budget, Parliament may consider additional grants. Excess grants are given when money has been spent on any service during a financial year in excess of the amount granted for that service in the budget for that year.

It is voted by the Lok Sabha after the financial year. Only if approval by the Public Accounts Committee to meet an unexpected demand upon resources and if the account is huge or of indefinite character, the vote on credit is resorted to like a blank cheque given to the executive by the Lok Sabha.

For special purposes that form no part of the current service of any financial year, exceptional grants can be made. Parliament makes token grants available if funds to meet the proposed expenditure on a new service are available by re-appropriation. A demand for the grant of a token sum (of Re 1) is submitted to the vote of the Lok Sabha and if assented, funds follow. Supplementary, additional, excess and exceptional grants and vote of credit are regulated by the same procedure which is applicable in the case of a regular budget.

The Appropriation Bill and Finance Bill after debate are put to vote on the floor of the Parliament sequentially. The Appropriation Bill comes first and then the Finance Bill has to make revenue provisions for the stipulated expenditure sanctioned by the Parliament. No amendment can be proposed to the Appropriation Bill in either house of the Parliament which will have the effect of varying the amount or altering the destination of any grant voted.

The Appropriation Bill becomes the Appropriation Act after it is assented to by the President. This Act authorizes the payments from the Consolidated Fund of India. If the government needs money to carry on its normal activities after 31st March, the Constitution authorizes the Lok Sabha to make grant in advance in respect to the estimated expenditure for a part of the financial year, pending the enactment of the Appropriation Bill. This 'Vote on Account' is passed after general discussion on budget and is generally granted for two months for an amount equivalent to one-sixth of the total estimation.

The Finance Bill when passed legalizes the income side of the budget. According to Provisional Collection of Taxes Act 1931, the Finance Bill in India has to be passed within 75 days. The bill gives effect to supplementary financial proposals for any period.

It is a money bill for procedural purposes and unlike the Appropriation Bill the members can move amendments to reject or reduce a tax in a prescribed manner. The proposals for new taxation require a previous consent of the President before presentation. The procedures for Railway Budget and Central Budget are identical.

Various Approaches to Budgeting

Budgeting is an essential part of any business. It allows a company to plan its financial resources and allocate them in a way that helps it achieve its goals and objectives.

By creating a budget, a company can set targets for its revenue and expenses, track its performance and make adjustments as needed to stay on track.

In this article, we will explore the different ways that companies can budget and how they can use these methods to improve their financial management.

Goals & Objectives

The first step in creating a budget is to determine the company's goals and objectives. This should be based on the company's strategic plan and should take into account the current economic environment and market conditions.

Once the goals and objectives have been established, the company can begin to allocate its resources accordingly.

Static Budget

One way to budget is through the use of a static budget. This type of budget is based on the assumption that the company's revenues and expenses will remain constant over a given period of time.

For example, a company might create a static budget for a quarter or a year.

This type of budget can be useful for companies that operate in stable environments where there is little fluctuation in revenues and expenses.

However, many businesses operate in dynamic environments where there can be significant changes in revenues and expenses.

In these cases, a static budget may not be the most effective way to plan and manage the company's finances.

In these situations, companies can use a flexible budget.

Flexible Budget

A flexible budget is a type of budget that takes into account changes in revenues and expenses. This type of budget is based on the assumption that the company's revenues and expenses will vary based on the level of activity or output.

For example, a company might create a flexible budget for a month or a quarter.

This type of budget can be useful for companies that operate in dynamic environments where there can be significant changes in revenues and expenses.

Zero-based Budget

Another way to budget is through the use of a zero-based budget. This type of budget is based on the assumption that the company should start from scratch and justify every expense.

In other words, every expense must be explicitly approved and allocated in the budget.

This type of budget can be useful for companies that want to closely control their expenses and ensure that they are being used in the most efficient and effective way possible.

Rolling Budget

A rolling budget is a type of budget that covers a set period of time, such as a quarter or a year and is regularly updated to reflect changes in the company's revenues and expenses.

This type of budget can be useful for companies that operate in dynamic environments where there can be significant changes in their revenues and expenses.

Unlike a static budget, which assumes that revenues and expenses will remain constant over a given period of time, a rolling budget takes into account changes in these variables and adjusts the budget accordingly.

This can help the company to more accurately plan and manage its financial resources and stay on track to achieve its goals and objectives.

Top-down Budget

A top-down budget is a type of budget that is created by top-level managers and then allocated to lower-level managers.

In this approach, top-level managers first establish the overall financial goals and objectives for the company and then determine how much money should be allocated to each department or division in order to achieve these goals.

This information is then passed down to lower-level managers, who use it to create their own budgets for their respective departments or divisions.

The advantage of a top-down budget is that it allows for a high-level view of the company's financial goals and how they will be achieved.

This can help to ensure that the company's resources are being allocated in a way that is aligned with its overall objectives.

However, some critics argue that a top-down budget can be inflexible and may not take into account the specific needs and challenges of individual departments or divisions.

As a result, some companies may choose to use a more bottom-up approach to budgeting, where lower-level managers are given more autonomy in determining how their budgets should be allocated.

Bottoms-up Budget

A bottom-up budget is a type of budget that is created by lower-level managers and then consolidated into a company-wide budget.

In this approach, individual managers in each department or division are responsible for creating their own budgets based on their specific needs and objectives.

These budgets are then consolidated into a larger, company-wide budget.

The advantage of a bottom-up budget is that it allows managers to take into account the specific needs and challenges of their departments or divisions.

This can help to ensure that the company's resources are being allocated in the most effective and efficient way possible.

However, some critics argue that a bottom-up budget can be less aligned with the company's overall financial goals and objectives and may not provide a comprehensive view of how the company's resources are being used.

Hybrid Budget

Since Top-down and Bottom-up have their critiques, how about both? Can you use a hybrid approach?

Yes, it is possible for a company to use a hybrid approach to budgeting that combines elements of both bottom-up and top-down budgeting.

In this approach, lower-level managers are given autonomy to create their own budgets based on the specific needs and challenges of their departments or divisions.

These budgets are then consolidated into a larger, company-wide budget that is reviewed and approved by top-level managers.

The advantage of a hybrid approach is that it allows for flexibility and customization at the lower levels, while still providing top-level managers with oversight and control over the company's overall financial goals and objectives.

This can help to ensure that the company's resources are being allocated in a way that is aligned with its overall strategy and priorities.

However, some critics argue that a hybrid approach can be more complex and time-consuming to implement and may not provide the level of control and visibility that some companies may need.

As a result, the best approach to budgeting will depend on the specific needs and goals of each individual company.

Importance of Ongoing Budget Monitoring and Adjustment

One important thing to keep in mind when it comes to budgeting is that it is not a one-time process.

Creating a budget is just the first step; it is equally important to regularly monitor and adjust the budget as needed to ensure that it remains relevant and effective.

This may involve tracking actual revenues and expenses, comparing them to the budgeted amounts and making adjustments as needed to stay on track.

By regularly reviewing and updating the budget, a company can ensure that it remains aligned with its goals and objectives and can make any necessary adjustments to its financial management strategy.

In Conclusion:

The Importance of Effective Budgeting in Business

Regardless of the type of budget that a company uses, there are several key steps that should be followed when creating a budget.

These include:

Identify the company's goals and objectives.

Determine the time period that the budget will cover (e.g., a quarter, a year, etc.).

Estimate the company's revenues and expenses.

Allocate resources to support the company's goals and objectives.

Monitor and adjust the budget as needed to stay on track.

In summary, budgeting is a crucial part of any business.

It allows a company to plan its financial resources and allocate them in a way that helps it achieve its goals and objectives.

There are several different methods that companies can use to budget, including static budgets, flexible budgets, zero-based budgets, top-down budgets, bottom-up budgets and hybrid budgets.

Regardless of the type of budget that a company uses, it is important to follow a set of key steps when creating a budget, such as identifying the company's goals and objectives, estimating its revenues and expenses and allocating resources to support these goals and objectives.

By doing so, a company can create a budget that is tailored to its specific needs and can help it to better manage its financial resources and achieve its desired outcomes.

CHAPTER FOUR

Citizen and Administration Interface

Public Service Delivery In India

The goal of public services is to provide social protection to the poor and vulnerable as well as to alleviate poverty. Public services help to reduce inequitable resource allocation and remedy past injustices such as caste prejudice and gender inequity.

Main challenges to public service delivery in India

(i) Large gaps exist in the country between the poor and the non-poor, with the poor suffering far more as a result of inadequate public service delivery.

(ii) Citizens tend to vote for leaders from their own community, caste or religion because of the culture of 'identity politics.'

(iii) The number of elected politicians with criminal records is on the rise which could stifle economic progress.

(iv) Politicians believe that providing help to citizens will result in increased electoral returns.

(v) Corruption is frequently cited as the root cause of governance problems.

(vi) The poor are ignorant to the benefits of good health and education.

(vii) In this age of social media, we have WhatsApp rumors and fake news.

(viii) The utilization of ICT services is plagued with administrative issues.

Policy measures
Community mobilisation

(i) Low-cost method of putting pressure on public officials to deliver.

(ii) Participation of women from poor, lower-caste, vulnerable households Self-Help Groups (SHGs).

Technology

(i) Technology can be used to keep track of service delivery and promote accountability.

(ii) The use of biometric identification and computerized benefit transfers has resulted in a decrease in program leakages.

(iii) Using ICT to enhance efficiency of health care delivery.

(iv) Increased teledensity and broadband penetration are required.

Cohesion and consensus among states

All of these public services are primarily provided by the state. Hence, cohesion and consensus among states should be promoted and laggard states need to be incentivised to undertake reforms.

Decentralisation

(i) Local governments, not top-down governments, may be better at conserving natural resources.

(ii) Regular training of public officials will help to strengthen the capacity of local governments.

Affirmative action

Improved access to public services for marginalised populations.

Performance-related pay

(i) Performance-based remuneration encourages public employees to put in more effort and as a result improves public service performance.

(ii) Non-monetary incentives can be a simple and effective way to reward good work e.g. transfers to preferred locations.

Way Forward

In the domain of bureaucratic reform, more research is required. Building strong accountability structures and media has an important role to play here. A forum for all media houses to come together and contribute to an informed debate on what is plaguing our public systems can be formed. Also, issues of last-mile access need to be tackled. By following these steps, the quality of public service delivery can be enhanced.

Essay on the benefits of Citizen-administration interface

Man evolved a system of regulating and even controlling his life when after discarding a life of isolation and loneliness he began co-existing with fellow human beings.

The development of the community thus induced him to contrive a pattern of governance to direct his affairs. From such a viewpoint, government can be considered as old as society itself-ushering government into society as well as society in government.

Of all the forms of government practised by mankind, democracy has been the youngest. Democracy in the modern institutional form, first originated in Great Britain but it is only in the present twentieth century that democracy is able to acquire its representative character.

This democracy in its earlier phase was an open-ended oligarchy. Blacks did not enjoy the right to vote. Women were enfranchised in various countries only between the two World Wars. France enfranchised its women as late as 1945.

Belgium conferred voting rights on its women in 1949 in a cross-cultural study on democracy conducted in 1951 by the United Nations Educationalist Scientific and Cultural Organisation (UNESCO), it triumphantly concluded: For the first time in history, democracy is claimed as the proper, ideal description of all systems of political and social organisation. Democracy proved to be an expanding phenomenon.

Democracy as visualised, even practised was political, its external symbols being periodic elections based on adult franchise with no discrimination based on religion, race, sex or beliefs. Freedom of expression was unabridged.

This conception of democracy was discovered to be narrow, weak and inadequate with the passage of time. Democracy in order to be viable and acceptable was to include and articulate social and economic concerns also. Society was moving from individualism to collectivism which could not but influence the agenda of democracy also.

Paradigm shift

Democracy is a dynamic, even demanding concept, never static in its contents and connotations. Since the eighties a new wave is in evidence of which the most notable feature is a shift from mere government to Governance. The latter is a broader concept covering themes like judicial review, due process, public interest litigation.

Newer Concerns such as ethics in administration, accountability, openness and client-friendliness etc. animate or inanimate public administrations among these new vibrations rank Responsive Administration.

The term became popular since 1946 when a conference of chief secretaries of states was organised in Delhi at the instance of the late Prime Minister. The Department given the responsibility of promoting this attribute is the Department of Administrative Reforms and Public Grievances in the Government of India.

Responsive Administration may not be confused with responsible government. These two terms are organically inter-linked and inter-twined. But they are separate. Responsible Government is a political concept and carries a definite connotation. It is a macro-concept. Responsive administration is basically animated at the cutting edge of public administration. It is micro level concept deriving its credibility and validity from the delivery system of a country's public administration. Responsive administration is best defined by Mahatma Gandhi.

Mahatma Gandhi said, 'I will give you a talisman. Whenever you are in doubt or when the self becomes too much with you, try the following expedient. Recall the face of the poorest and the most helpless man whom you may have seen and ask yourself if the step you contemplate is going to be of any use to him.

Will it restore him to a control over his own life and destiny? In other words, will it lead to Swaraj or self-rule for the hungry and spiritually starving millions of our countrymen? Then you will find your doubts and yourself melting away'.

Responsive administration is an apparently moral concept in public administration in as much as it calls for public functionaries and accountability directly to the people. Responsive administration entails mechanism of redressal of grievances also.

Mahatma's talisman, thus, is the acid test of responsive administration. Citizen empowerment constitutes the single most critical element of responsive administration.

Hindrance

The problem of administrative responsiveness is to be addressed within the larger social context. The present national scenario has to reckon with certain parameters of which the two are of paramount concern.

1. First is economic liberalisation to which India is firmly committed since the nineties.

2. The second parameter in the governing framework is the constitutionalisation of local government as a result of the 73rd and 74th constitutional amendments. Responsiveness is to be operationalised within this larger context.

3. Contents of Responsive Administration: Citizen satisfaction is also described by a catchy expression such as 'service with a smile, not by a mile'. Since seventies particularly, public administration is showing growing-interest in customers (or consumer) satisfaction measured in the quality of service delivery, client perception of service quality and consumer satisfaction.

Quality of service in public administration is reported to be poor even in industrialised countries of the West and what is worse it is deteriorating despite the existence of free market. In developing countries like India, the quality of services is appalling.

4. Responsive administration explicitly acknowledges the citizen-sovereignty in administrative dealings and relationships. This orientation is its chief component, the other being well-defined constitutional mechanisms for redressal of citizen's grievances.

Public administration is already seeing the emergence of devices like representative bureaucracy, lok adalats, consumer courts, citizens' Charter etc. These must be strengthened and made effective. Citizens' charter laid down a code of practice in delivery systems.

It seeks to re-define the citizen as a customer and improves responsiveness and performance in the public services. It establishes minimum standards of public service reflecting the following six principles of social rights: fair treatment, entitlement, participation, openness, public administration and cooperation.

Excellence of administration

Responsive administration is a concept which needs emulation in all administrations. Its need is however much more obvious in a developing country like India with its long colonial background resting on stiff-necked bureaucracy, attributes of responsive administration is a must.

Thus permeate all levels and sectors of public administration but the need for citizen-friendly administration is most pressing at the cutting edge of administration: the countless points where administration and citizen daily meet.

At present, in most parts of the country, the contact points between citizen and administration are virtually a hacking point: a point of apparently endless harassment for the people, especially those who are on the fringe of development.

This, among others, calls for attitudinal change in the country's bureaucracy and nowhere perhaps it is more necessary than in those constituting field of administration.

The field level professionals are called upon to cultivate citizen-oriented attitudes. In addition, they must also possess and continually cultivate higher measures of administrative skills and subject matter capabilities.

This calls for larger- scale changes in the public personnel practices and strengthening of the present tenure system. District administration must need to be rejuvenated and activated to enlist the good will of the local people.

Responsive administration is ensured in what has come to be known as the Batho Pele Principles. These principles put the citizens first in a search for efficient public service delivery. These principles were proclaimed by South Africa in 1997. These are:

1. Service Standard: Citizens should be told what level and quality of public services, they will receive so that they are aware of what to expect.

2. Access: All citizens should have equal access to the services, which they are entitled, for example, increasing access to public services for those who have not previously received them. Many people who like in remote areas can be reached by setting up mobile units and redeploying facilities and resources closer to those in greatest need.

3. Ensuring Courtesy: Citizens should be treated with courtesy and consideration.

4. Providing More and Better Information : Citizens should be given full, accurate information about the public services they are entitled to receive, especially those who have previously been excluded from the provision of public services.

5. Increasing Openness and Transparency: Citizens should be told how national and provincial departments are run, how much they cost and who is in charge.

6. Remedying Mistake and Failures (Redress): If the promised standard of service is not delivered, citizens should be offered an apology, a full explanation and a speedy and effective remedy and when complaints are made, citizens should receive a sympathetic, positive response.

7. Getting the Best Possible Value for Money: Public services should be provided economically and efficiently in order to give citizens the best possible value for money.

8. Consolation: Citizens should be consulted about the level and quality of the public services they receive and wherever possible, should be given a chance about the services that are offered. It is important that consolations not only cover aspects about services currently provided but also about the services of new basic services to those who lack them. In that way, consultation can help to foster a more participative and cooperative relationship between the providers and receivers of public services.

Policy-making should show sensitiveness to citizen's problems and must not be influenced by extra national interests. Here, a mention must be made of the new economic policy underway since 1990 requiring cultivation of new skills, knowledge and orientations and new equilibrium between administration and the people.

Grievance Redressal in India - An Overview

1. Grievance Redressal Mechanism is an important cog in the wheel of any Government.

2. Without efficient grievance redressal mechanisms, the Government and its administration can never be accountable and effective.

3. In Democracy, citizens make the Government and hold them accountable.

4. Some of the public grievances against the Government could be shortage of food, overcrowded public transport, late running of trains, etc.

Grievances of Citizens in India - Different Types

We can classify public grievances into different categories which are mentioned below:

Grievances against Policies

1. Citizens may have grievances against the policies of the Government which may affect a large group of people.

2. Such grievances are raised in the media and legislatures.

Grievances due to Maladministration

1. This grievance arises when the Government policies are not implemented efficiently by the administration due to various issues like lack of coordination between different departments or agencies or may be due to inefficiency of officials stemming from heavy workload.

Grievances due to Corruption

1. This arises due to lack of integrity among officials working in the administration. For many years India is known for its high levels of corruption. For many years the public has been suffering due to rampant corruption at all levels. However there are efforts from the current Government to control corruption.

Grievances in Rural Areas

Majority of the population in India resides in rural areas. The grievances faced by them are given below:

1. Non-availability of supplies - Grievances due to intermittent supply of essential commodities like electricity, seeds, pesticides, fertilizers, medicines, etc. Instead of making sure the supplies reach intended beneficiaries, it gets leaked into black markets for profiteering.

2. Delay in Supplies or Services - This happens due to inefficient public distribution systems.

3. Harassment - Many villagers at the hands of officials when they wanted to avail medical, administrative and agricultural services.

Grievance Redressal - Nodal Agencies & Other Mechanisms

The two most important nodal agencies that are responsible for addressing grievances at the Central Government are listed below:

1. Department of Administrative Reforms and Public Grievances (DARPG) - It functions under the Ministry of Personnel, Public Grievances and Pensions.

2. Directorate of Public Grievances - It is part of Cabinet Secretariat.

Department of Administrative Reforms and Public Grievances (DARPG)

1. The primary role of this department is to plan and implement citizen centric measures in the domain of public grievances and carry out administrative reforms so that the Government is in a position to deliver quality public services without any obstacles.
2. The grievances received will be forwarded to the respective ministries, departments and state governments. The cases will be followed till it is closed.

Directorate of Public Grievances (DPG)
1. It was set up in the Cabinet Secretariat in 1988. They handle complaints pertaining to 16 Central Government Organisations.

Ombudsman

This concept came from Sweden. It means an officer appointed by the Legislature to handle complaints against a service or administrative authority. In India, Government has appointed Ombudsmen to resolve grievances in the following sectors:
　1. Insurance Ombudsman
2. Banking Ombudsman
3. Income Tax Ombudsman

Lokpal

Lokpal was established under the Lokpal and Lokayuktas Act 2013 to investigate corruption against public functionaries, even the Prime Minister. Lokpal can order investigation from its internal inquiry wing, Central Bureau Investigation (CBI) and Chief Vigilance Commission (CVC).

Tribunals

Tribunals are formed to address delays in disposal of cases in courts. These are quasi-judicial institutions. Some of the most important tribunals are mentioned below:
1. Central Administrative Tribunal (CAT)
2. Railway Claims Tribunal
3. Debt Recovery Tribunal
4. Customs, Excise and Service Tax Tribunal
5. Income Tax Appellate Tribunal
6. Labour Tribunal

Committee on Petitions - Parliamentary Committee

This is a Parliamentary Committee which works on redressing grievances of the public, a citizen can submit petitions to secure redress against grievances.

E-Governance - To Address Public Grievances

The current Government has been working on addressing the public grievances by utilising Information and Communications Technology (ICT). Some of the noteworthy efforts of the Government to implement E-governance to reduce Public Grievances in a timely manner has been mentioned below:

1. Central Public Grievance Redress and Monitoring System (CPGRAMS) - It is an integrated online grievance redressal and monitoring system developed by National Informatics Centre (NIC) in collaboration with DARPG and DPG. Citizens can lodge complaints and monitor the status of their complaints through CPGRAMS. This system was developed in 2007.

2. Pro-Active Governance and Timely Implementation (PRAGATI) - It is a multi-modal and multi-purpose grievance redressal system designed by the Prime Minister's Office (PMO) and NIC. It increases the cooperation and coordination between Union Government and State Government in addressing the grievances and monitoring government schemes.

3. E-Nivaran - It was launched by the Central Board of Direct Taxes for online redressal of grievances related to taxpayers. The taxpayers can register and track their grievances in this system.

4. Unified Mobile Application for New-Age Governance (UMANG) - It is a single platform through which citizens across India can access e-governance services, starting from Central Government to local government bodies.

5. MyGov - It is a platform launched in 2014 to disseminate information by the Government and Government can seek public opinion.

6. Nivaran - It is an online portal launched by the Indian Railways in 2016 to address the grievances of lakhs of Railway Employees.

7. Integrated Grievance Redressal Mechanism (INGRAM) - It is a portal launched by the Ministry of Consumer Affairs to address grievances of the public when they purchase any goods or services.

8. Mera Aspataal (My Hospital) - It was an app and portal launched by the Ministry of Health in 2017 under the National Health Mission. It was to capture patient feedback for the services received at the Government Hospitals. This is to help the Government enhance the quality of health care services provided across public facilities.

Other Citizens Grievance Redressal Mechanisms

1. Right to Information Act - This act was passed in 2005. It empowers the citizens to ask any questions to the Government, seek information, obtain Government documents and inspect Government works. This act is to not only empower citizens but also promote transparency and accountability in the functioning of Government.

2. Citizens Charter - The task of formulating and opertionalising Citizens Charter was undertaken by DARPG. The idea was to bring in transparency in public services and to correct things when they go wrong. The idea of Citizen Charter was first pioneered in the United Kingdom in 1991 with focus on public services. However there have been many loopholes in the citizens charter which needs to be fixed.

3. Gram Sabha - Conducted at village levels to address the grievances of village community members.

4. Senior Citizen Act - It has been passed to address the grievances of senior citizens.

5. Hostels Act - This has been passed to address the grievances of working women.

Sevottam

1. This is a model proposed by the 2nd Administrative Reforms Commission.

2. When translated into English, Sevottam means Excellent Service.

3. This would provide a standard model for grievance redressal mechanisms. It will plug the loopholes of the Citizen Charter.

4. Sevottam focuses on improving the quality of service delivered to the citizens.

Sevottam - Focus Areas

Sevottam will work on rectifying problems in the following three main domains:

1. Public Grievance Mechanism

2. Citizen Charter
3. Service Delivery

Administrative Reforms Commission (ARC) - 2 Commissions

Administrative Reforms Commission (ARC) is the committee appointed by the Government of India for giving recommendations to reform the Public Administration System in India. So far there have been 2 Administrative Reforms Commissions. The details are shared below:

1st Administrative Reforms Commission (ARC)

1. The 1st ARC was established on 5th January 1966.
   2. The commission was chaired by Morarji Desai and was later chaired by K. Hanumanthaiah.

Mandate of 1st ARC

1. They were tasked with the mandate to suggest measures to improve financial, personnel, economic, district and agricultural administrations.
2. The administrations concerning Defence, Intelligence, External Affairs and Railways were excluded from the purview of 2nd ARC.

2nd Administrative Reforms Commission (ARC)

1. 2nd ARC was constituted on 31st August 2015.
2. Veerappa Moily was the chairman of the 2nd ARC.
3. It was tasked to revamp the public administrative system.

2nd ARC Report

The 2nd ARC submitted 15 reports covering the following areas
1. Right to Information (RTI)
2. Ethics in Governance
3. Local Governance
4. Public Administration
5. E-Governance
6. Combating Terrorism.

Right to Information Act 2005

The RTI Act 2005 is a significant act introduced in the constitution of India, which allows every individual to seek and receive information related to any issue regardless of the boundaries. The Right to Information Act was enacted by the Indian parliament to provide citizens with access to records held by the central and state governments. This act was passed by the parliament on June 2005 and it came into force in October 2005. The RTI Act 2005 provides a mechanism to develop and ensure accountability and transparency in line with Article 19(1)(a) of the constitution.

What is RTI Act 2005?

The Right to Information or RTI Act 2005 is a fundamental right enshrined in Article 19(1) of Part 3 of the Indian Constitution. In the Raj Narayan vs Uttar Pradesh State case, the Supreme Court ruled that the right to information is a fundamental right and it is the citizen's right to know about the workings of the government.

The Right to Information Act was passed on June 15, 2005 and implemented on October 12, 2005. It is a legal right. The credit for this act goes to Aruna Roy. The RTI Act 2005 replaces the Freedom of Information Act 2002. It also has a constitutional provision under article 19(1)a (which is the right to freedom of speech and expression) of the fundamental rights of the constitution. Sweden was the first country to implement the RTI Act.

Right to Information Act, 2005

The RTI Act 2005 is a tool to establish accountability and transparency in governance and is helpful in reducing corruption. It replaced the Freedom of information act 2002 to set up a practical regime of the right to information for every citizen.

Objectives of RTI Act 2005

The Objectives of the Right to Information Act 2005 are as follows:

To establish good governance, that is Ramraj, by empowering the citizens of the country to question the government.

The RTI Act 2005 helps to promote transparency, accountability and responsibility in the working of the government of the country.

It is very fruitful in reducing corruption in the country and working for the benefit of the citizens in a better way.

It also helps in changing the attitude of government officials toward ordinary citizens. RTI Act makes government officials more responsible for their duties.

Salient Features of RTI Act 2005

The RTI Act 2005 has a total of 31 sections, 6 chapters and two schedules. Some salient features of the Right to Information Act are as follows:

Under its provision, any citizen of India may request information from a public authority. The required information needs to be replied to within 30 days.

The request for information on any issue from the public authority is required to be submitted to the Public Information officer at the centre or in the State.

The RTI Act encourages every government body to make their offices transparent by computerizing their records for the wide dissemination of the information to the public.

Jammu and Kashmir will not come under the RTI Act 2005. However, it has a separate 2009 Act.

The restrictions imposed by the Official Secrets Act 1923 were relaxed by this act.

The Act has established a three-tier structure for enforcing the right to information guaranteed under the Act. The three Levels are – Public Information Officer, First Appellate Authority and Central Information Commission (CIC).

In case of non-receipt of information within 30 days, the individual requiring information may file an appeal. The Appellate Authority must reply within 30 days or in 45 days in exceptional cases.

The individual may file 2nd appeal within 90 days in case of non-supply of information.

The public authorities applicable under the RTI act are all Constitutional bodies at centre and state (Legislature, Executive, Judiciary), bodies/NGOs owned/financed by the government and privatized public utility companies.

The public authorities excluded under RTI are agencies of the state specified through notification, Central Intelligence and Security Agencies.

The Central Information Commission shall consist of one Chief Information Commissioner and up to 10 Central Information Commissioners.

The Chief Information Commissioner will have a term of five years from the date of entering his office. She/He shall not be entitled to reappointment to that post.

Section 8 deals with public authorities which have been granted an exemption under this act.

Importance of RTI (Right to Information Act)

RTI Act 2005 allowed the common people to know about what is happening in the country by giving them the power to question the government about their work, schemes, etc.

The act also helps farmers by providing them with solutions to their problems like soil, pest problems, etc.

It helps in solving the cases pending in the courts.

It empowers the information commission to be the highest authority of the country with the power to order any office in the country to provide information as per the provision of the RTI Act 2005 and also empowers the commission to punish the violation of the RTI.

It also helps vulnerable sections of society by helping them to know their rights.

Need for RTI Act 2005

The right to information is essential in today's world because it promotes transparency and accountability in government functions.

The weaker and vulnerable sections of society are also empowered by this RTI Act which gives them the power to seek information about the policies that are being run for them and from which they will benefit.

The RTI Act 2005 has already revealed major corruption, such as the Common Health Game Organization and the 2G spectrum scam.

Now government officials do not discriminate against citizens based on race, caste or sex as they know if they do something which is against civil rights. He will take action and this is possible just because of the Right to Information Act.

Right to Information is a Fundamental Right

There are six fundamental rights included in the Indian Constitution under Articles 12 to 35, Part 3 of the Constitution. The Right to Information is a fundamental right under Article 19(1)(a), which is the right to freedom of speech and expression. It was implemented in 2005.

Process of filing the RTI

According to the Right to Information Act, any person may file a written request to the Public Information Officer (PIO), who is established by the authorities to seek the information.

The officer must give the information sought by the applicant and if he does not get the information, then he has the option to file a request in front of the state or Central Information Commission.

There is also a provision for a time limit in the RTI Act 2005 so that the process can be done quickly.

Different time limits are prescribed for different situations.

When an applicant seeks information from any public information officer, then they must reply to the applicant within a time limit of 30 days and for any application seeking information from assistant public information officers, then, in this case, the time limit is to provide information within 35 days.

The application can be transferred to another public information officer in 30 days.

Any applicant seeking information regarding corruption or any kind of violation of human rights, which are covered under schedule 2 of the RTI Act, must be given within 45 days with permission of the Central Information Commission.

Challenges of the RTI Act 2005

According to a recent study, only 36 per cent of people in rural areas and 38 per cent of people in urban areas have heard of the RTI Act. The other challenges of the Right to Information Act 2005 are as follows:

The participation of women in the act is not sufficient for a progressive and empowered society.

The data shows that around 45% of public information officers did not get any training while joining the post.

There has been a tendency of poor record-keeping practices by the central and state government offices. This violates section 4 of the RTI Act 2005.

The pendency of cases is a clear indication of the casual approach of the government towards RTI.

There is a lack of appropriate infrastructure and a huge deficiency in staff required for running Information Commissions.

The dilution of the whistle-blower protection act is a cause of concern.

The security and protection of RTI activists in the course of their work is a cause of concern.

The non-inclusion of the Judiciary and political parties creates suspicion in mind and creates a hurdle in the fight towards making the system more transparent and accountable.

The recent changes will create political patronage in the selection of Information Commissioners and will lead to the dilution of the main purpose of the RTI act.

Right to Information Act Amendment

Earlier, the Chief Information Commissioner at the centre and state levels were appointed for a 5-year term under the RTI Act 2005. But according to the RTI Amendment Act 2019, now, the tenure of the Chief Information Commissioner in the centre and state will be notified by the union government.

Earlier, according to the RTI Act 2005, the salaries of the Chief Information Commissioner and the Information Commissioners were equal to the salary of the chief election commissioner and the election commissioners, but after the amendment now, the central and the state Chief Information Commissioner and information commissioners salary, allowances and other terms and condition of the employment shall be made by the central government.

RTI Amendment Act 2019 removes the provision that at the time of appointment of the Chief Information Commissioner and Information Commissioners at the Central and the State level, receiving a pension or any other retirement benefits for the previous government services, then their salary will be reduced by an amount equal to the pension.

Lokpal and Lokayukta - The Law and Its Importance

State and Corription

A government is established for bettering the standard of living of the people it governs and thus, it is rightly inferred that the with the prosperity of the people lies the security, strength and stability of the government and democracy.

The government performs an administrative function and plays a key role in the socio-economic activities in the state. Ethical conduct is always a genuine concern. This is because such power has scope to be misused.

Such misuse of power done with the purpose of either not carrying out the prescribed task or doing the task in a perverted way so as to gain a personal benefit out of the same while utilizing the powers of the government hollows the belief of the people in the government and leads to corruption.

Corruption however, is not just an individual's conduct. While it may stem from the action of one the causes of corruption are deep rooted in the policy of a country, its bureaucracy, political developments and social history of a country. It must be noted that corruption is a collective effort between groups and thus, involves going beyond private gains towards other vested interests within the political system. This practice, thrives where there is weaker accountability and the person involved has a wider discretion of powers.

Although corruption takes many forms and is ubiquitous in nature, the acts of misconduct and maladministration, we are referring to are those of politicians, government ministers, civil servants and other elected members who abuse the powers of their office to decide on the laws, regulations or the allocation of resources in society. Such corruption is also referred as political corruption and in India about five players can be identified for running this vicious cycle of corruption:

1. The 'Neta' or the corrupt politician;
2. The 'Babu' or the corrupt bureaucrat;
3. The 'Lala' or the corrupting businessman;
4. The 'Jhola' or the corrupt NGO; and
5. The 'Dada' or the criminal of the underworld.

Recognizing that the role of the government is for the welfare of the people it governs, corrupt actions diminish the satisfaction of the people which further leads to alienation. To prevent reaching the final outcome and for building a satisfied population, the role of the government is defined with two objectives:

- To make the administration free from corruption and maladministration.
- To make it responsive to the needs of the people.

Need and Role of Ombudsman

Surprisingly, there are already established means within the current system of governance to hold the government accountable such as the legislature, the judiciary, the administrative agencies themselves, other political parties and the press. However, each one of them have certain shortfalls on the matter.

For instance, in the house of parliament there exists a Committee of Public Undertaking which reports on the country's financial and economics standing. Then there is the Committee on Government Assurances which that reports on the status of the assurances given by the Ministers and there also exists the Committee of Petitions that looks at the complaints and petitions raised by the netizens. The problem with this means however, is the lack of awareness on the part of the citizens as they may not have the knowledge about the existence of such an approach.

An argument could be made for the legislature and the judiciary. However, in the case of the legislator are usually engaged in the matter of policy making to appease these citizens and hence, they do not have time to address the complaints of individual citizens. In the case of the judiciary the remedies available to the petitioner are (i) the quashing of the order (ii) prosecution of the offending servant and lastly, the writ jurisdiction of the High Court and the Supreme Court for quashing orders, or command duty to be done from the public servant. However, this power has been diluted due to the creation of tribunals and also by transferring certain powers to certain administrative officials therefore no remedy can be provided by the courts if such issue does not fall under appellate jurisdiction unless it is specially provided under relevant statute or if it falls under Article 136 of the constitution granting special leave to the Supreme Court. Another problem that arises is the cost and time taken for the entire proceeding to get over.

To solve this problem the Administration Reforms Commission which was headed by Mr. Morarji Desai in its interim report "Problems of redress of citizen grievances" recommended the establishment of two new institutions known as "Lokpal" and "Lokayukta" for India. The idea of creating an "Ombudsman" was borrowed from Sweden where this institution is given powers to enquire, investigate and prosecute on the basis of the complaints of the citizens the maladministration of the government departments.

The Ombudsman was given certain powers under Swedish Law. Such as he was independent from the executive government and the parliament and he may apart from the complaints received take suo motu cognizance of matters and investigate on his own and while investigating he gets access to all the documents from the authorities concerned and he may examine the accused orally himself. The ombudsman was required to make a report on an yearly basis for the work done and is submitted to a committee of the Legislature who then makes a report to the Parliament and if the work of the Ombudsman is considered not upto the standard then the committee may even recommend his removal.

Salient Features of the Lokpal and Lokayuktas Act, 2013

In India, the establishment of an Ombudsman institution has happened through the Lokpal and Lokayuktas Act, 2013 which was enacted in the year 2014. The act provides the following key details:

➢ Appointment

The Lokpal chairman and members can hold office for a period of 5 years or till they attain the age of 70 years, whichever is earlier. The members and the chairman of Lokpal are appointed by the president on the recommendation of a selection committee.

The selection committee consists of-

- The Prime Minister of India (chairperson);
- The Speaker of Lok Sabha;
- The Leader of Opposition in Lok Sabha;
- The Chief Justice of India or any Judge nominated by Chief Justice of India;
- One eminent jurist.

➢ Investigative powers

The Lokpal on the receipt of a complaint may order a-

1. Preliminary inquiry against any public servant by its Inquiry Wing or any agency (including the Delhi Special Police Establishment) to ascertain whether there exists a prima facie case for proceeding in the matter.

2. Investigation by any agency (including the Delhi Special Police Establishment) when there exists a prima facie case jurisdiction

A Lokpal may inquire or start an investigation on the allegation of a complainant against the following people:

- Prime Minister and the other Ministers,
- Members of Parliament,
- Groups A, B, C and D officers,
- Officials of Central Government,
- Every person who is or has been in charge (director/manager/secretary) of a body or a society set up by the act of central government,
- Any society or body financed or controlled by the central government,
- Any person involved in act of abetting, bribe giving or bribe-taking.

Things needed to file a Lokpal complaint

The procedure to file a Lokpal Complaint is defined under the Lokpal Rules, 2020.

A complaint must necessarily contain the following-

1. Details regarding the alleged commission of offence by the public servant.

2. The complaint to be made in any language included in the Eighth Schedule of the constitution.

3. A copy of the address proof of the complainant.

4. A registration or incorporation certificate if, in case the complaint is being made on behalf of an organization or if it is a board, body, corporation, company, limited liability partnership, authority, society, association of persons or trust.

5. A copy of an authorization certificate if, in case the complaint is being made on behalf of an organization or if it is a board, body, corporation, company, limited liability partnership, authority, society, association of persons or trust.

6. An Affidavit in the form as specified in the Part D of the Annexure.

7. Lastly, duly signed detailed statement making out the allegation.

Citizen's Charter

The citizen's charter is a document that outlines the service commitment of organizations or service providers towards providing quality, high-standard services, including mechanisms for grievance redressal.

The Citizen's Charter is a voluntary and written document that spells out the service provider's efforts taken to focus on their commitment towards fulfilling the needs of the citizens/customers.

It also includes how citizens can redress any grievances.

It includes what the citizens can expect out of the service provider.

The concept is that the charter preserves the trust between the service provider and the citizens/users.

The concept of a citizen's charter was initiated by former British Prime Minister John Major in the year 1991. It was started as a national programme intended to improve the quality of public services. In 1998, in the UK, the concept was renamed 'Services First'.

Principles of Citizen's Charter (As originally framed)

Quality – Improving service quality.

Choice – Wherever possible.

Standards – Specifically mention what to expect and how to go about if standards are not met.

Value – For taxpayers' money.

Accountability – At the level of the individual and the organization.

Transparency – Transparency in rules/schemes/procedures/grievances.

After the adoption by the UK, several other countries adopted a citizen's charter under different names and forms. The basic idea was the same, however, to enhance the quality of services offered to the public and have transparency and accountability in public services.

The 6 principles as laid out by the government in the UK, were later elaborated in 1998. The Labour government, then, brought out the following nine principles of Service Delivery:

Set standards of service

Be open and provide full information

Consult and involve

Encourage access and the promotion of choice

Treat all fairly

Put things right when they go wrong

Use resources effectively

Innovate and improve

Work with other providers

Citizen's Charter in India

In India, the concept of citizen's charter was first adopted at a 'Conference of Chief Ministers of various States and Union Territories' held in May 1997 in the national capital.

A major outcome of the conference was a decision to formulate Citizen's Charters by the central and state governments, beginning with sectors with a large public interface such as the railways, telecom, posts, PDS, etc.

The charters were mandated to include service standards, the time limit that the people can expect to be served, mechanisms for redressing grievances and a provision for unbiased scrutiny by consumer/citizen groups.

The task of coordination, formulation and operationalization of citizen's charters are done by the Department of Administrative Reforms and Public Grievances (DARPG).

In India, in this context, citizens can mean not only citizens but also all stakeholders such as customers, clients, beneficiaries, ministries/departments/organizations, state/UT governments, etc.

The Indian model of citizen's charter is an adaptation from the UK model. One additional component of the charter in the Indian version is the inclusion of the point 'expectation from clients'.

The DARPG website lists more than 700 charters adopted by various government agencies across India.

The Right of Citizens for Time Bound Delivery of Goods and Services and Redressal of their Grievances Bill, 2011 (Citizens Charter) was introduced in the Lok Sabha in December 2011. It was referred to a Standing Committee which submitted its report in 2012. The bill, however, lapsed due to the dissolution of the Lok Sabha in 2014.

Citizen's charters are not legally enforceable documents. They are just guidelines to enhance service delivery to citizens.

Citizen's Charter Components

A good citizen's charter should include the following details:

Organization's vision and mission statements.

A business carried out and other such details of the organization.

Explain who are citizens and clients.

Statement of services including quality, time-frame, etc. offered to citizens and how to get those services.

Grievance redressal mechanisms.

Expectations from citizens/clients.

Additional commitments like the amount of compensation in case of service delivery failure.

Other Elements of a Good Citizen's Charter

Should be in simple language

The focus should be on the requirements of the customers

There should be periodic review

Reliability should be imbibed – that is, consistency in performance/delivery

Objectives of Citizen's Charters

The basic objective of the citizen's charters is to empower citizens through the delivery of public services.

Improve the quality of public services.

Ensuring transparency and right to information.

Save the time of both the customer and the service provider.

Have clear targets for all levels of services.

Features of Citizen's Charters

The salient features of a citizen's charter are given below:

Lays down clear standards for the delivery of services. The standards should be measurable, time-bound, relevant, specific and accurate.

Gives full information about the services, in simple language, as to what services are available, level of quality to expect, grievance mechanism, etc.

Wherever possible, the charter should offer a choice of services to the clients.

It should also be made with regular consultation with all stakeholders including customers to ascertain the quality standards.

It should encourage a culture of courtesy and helpfulness among the personnel of the service provider.

Significance of Citizen's Charters

Citizen's charters are significant in that they empower citizens when it comes to public services.

It boosts accountability in the delivery of public services.

It enhances good governance.

It improves the effectiveness of organizations by having measurable standards.

It augments the quality of services delivered by incorporating an internal and external monitoring entity.

Being citizen-centric, it creates a professional and customer-oriented environment for the delivery of services.

It also helps boost the morale of the staff.

It enhances transparency and openness.

However, there are some drawbacks also associated with these charters. They are mentioned in the below section.

Challenges faced in implementing Citizen's Charters in India

A general perception is that these are seen as a mere formality. There is no involvement from the personnel and citizens and the whole exercise is carried out because it was a command from the top.

It can overburden organizations and government agencies. It might also divert the attention of the personnel from their work.

Improper training of the staff leads to the charter being merely drafted and not implemented properly.

In certain cases, unrealistic charters are drafted. This can lead to expectations not being met.

The citizen's charter is not legally enforceable. This has made them ineffective in a real sense.

Generally, the charters are drafted unilaterally by the service provider without taking into consideration the opinions and feedback of the customers. NGOs are also not consulted.

There is also a lack of infrastructure in the country to go side-by-side with this initiative.

There is a need for a team effort to implement the charter in its true spirit. There is a hierarchy gap between officers and field staff, which leads to a lack of coordination and motivation.

The charters are not periodically revised.

It is also seen that the needs of the disabled and senior citizens are not taken into account while framing.

Sometimes, the rules and procedures are found to be excessively complicated.

There is a lack of awareness among the public about citizen's charters.

Standards defined are generally not measurable making the whole exercise ineffective.

It is seen that organizations themselves are not keen to implement and adhere to their charters.

There is a tendency to have a uniform citizen's charter for all agencies, departments, etc. under the same parent organization. The charter should be customized as per the needs and functioning of the particular office/agency.

There are only a few more than 700 charters adopted in the country. It is still a long way to go in terms of universal charter adoption.

2nd ARC Recommendations

The Second Administrative Reforms Commission (ARC) had made recommendations to improve the effectiveness of citizen's charters. Some of the recommendations are:

They should specify the remedy/compensation in the case of any default in meeting the standards mentioned in the charters.

Charters should restrict a few promises that can be kept rather than have a long unfulfilled list.

Before making a charter, the organization should restructure its set-up and processes.

There should not be a uniform charter across organizations. They should be local and customized.

All stakeholders must be kept on board while drafting the charters.

Commitments made should be firm and there should be a citizen-friendly redressal mechanism.

Officers should be held accountable if commitments made are not fulfilled.

The citizen's charters should be reviewed and revised regularly.

Reforms for Citizen Charter to make them Effective

Not everyone fits in the same mold: Citizen Charter should be formulated as a decentralized activity with the head office providing only broad guidelines.

Wide consultation process: Formulation of Citizen Charter should be done after extensive consultations within the organization followed by meaningful dialogue with civil society.

Commitments of the firms should be made: Citizen Charter should be precise and must make firm commitments of service delivery standards to the citizens or consumers in quantifiable terms wherever possible.

Provide Redressal mechanism in case of default: Citizen charter should clearly lay down the relief which the organization is bound to provide if it has defaulted on the promised standards of delivery.

Periodic evaluation: A citizen charter should be evaluated from time to time preferably through an external agency.

Officers to be held accountable for results: In cases where there is a default in adhering to the Citizen Charter, fix specific responsibility.

Society should be a part of it: To help in improvement in the contents of the Charter, Civil Society should be included in it. They should be a part of the process, its adherence as well as in educating the citizens about the importance of the vital mechanism of the Citizen Charter.

Way Forward

A Citizens' Charter is a means to an end it cannot be an end in itself. It is a tool to ensure that the citizen is always at the heart of any service delivery mechanism.

Drawing from best practice models such as the Sevottam Model (a Service Delivery Excellence Model) can help Citizen's Charter in becoming more citizen-centric.

Questions related to Citizen's Charter

Q. When was Citizen Charter introduced in India?

Ans. It was introduced in India in 1997.

Q. Why is a Citizen Charter important?

Ans. It is an important tool in public administration that can enhance the quality of service offered to citizens, improve transparency, and foster trust in the system.

Q. What is the Citizen Charter Act?

Ans. The Citizen's Charter and Grievance Redressal Bill 2011 is also known as the Right of Citizens for Time Bound Delivery of Goods and Services and Redressal of their Grievances Bill, 2011. This was introduced in Parliament in 2011 but the bill has now lapsed.

E-Governance: Meaning, Objectives, Features, And 4 Types

One of the most modern initiatives to establish good governance is e-governance. At present, the features of e-governance are observed in almost all developed or underdeveloped and developing countries for fostering their developmental process. So its importance in today's world is immense.

What is E-Governance or Electronic Governance?

A new paradigm shift has been developed in the field of governance by the application of ICT in the processes of governing called Electronic-Governance or E-Governance.

E-governance raises the transparency, accountability, efficiency and effectiveness and inclusiveness in the governing process in terms of reliable access to the information within government, between government, national, state, municipal and local level governments, citizens and businesses and empowers business through access and use of information.

The main focus of the E-Governance or electronic governance is to provide transparent, equitable and accountable service delivery to the citizens. The aim of the e-governance facilitates and improves the quality of governance and ensures people's participation in the governing process through electronic means like e-mail, websites, SMS connectivity and others.

E-governance is not just about government websites or e-mail or financial transactions. "It will change how citizens relate to government as much as it changes how citizens relate to each other". It also refers to the utilization of IT in the country's democratic processes itself such as the election.

E-governance is about the use of ICT for steering the citizens and promoting the public service. It includes a pragmatic application and usage of ICT for delivering efficient and cost effective services and information and knowledge to the citizens being governed, thereby realizing the vast potential of the government to serve the citizens. It made correlations between state and society, government and people, people to people, governance and society.

Objectives of E Governance

The objectives of e governance are as follows-

One of the basic objectives of e-governance is to make every information of the government available to all in the public interest.

One of its goals is to create a cooperative structure between the government and the people and to seek help and advice from the people, to make the government aware of the problems of the people.

To increase and encourage people's participation in the governance process.

E-Governance improves the country's information and communication technology and electronic media with the aim of strengthening the country's economy by keeping governments, people and businesses in tune with the modern world.

One of its main objectives is to establish transparency and accountability in the governance process.

To reduce government spending on information and services.

Features of E Governance

It has been proven from the concept of e-governance that it is a powerful means of public service in the present era. Some of its features can be found by observing the functioning of e-governance.

De bureaucratization: Due to e-governance, the gap between the people and the government in all the services of the government is narrowing and the dependence of the people on the bureaucracy is also greatly reduced.

E-Services: Its main feature is the provision of services through the Internet. As a result, we get G2C, G2B, G2E, etc. services. This is already discussed in the section of 'types of governance'.

International Services: through e-governance, all the essential services can be delivered to the citizens who are living outside of their country for job purposes or any other reasons.

It enhances the right to express to the citizens. Using the means of e-governance anyone can share their views with the government on any bill or act or decision taken by the government.

Economic Development: With the introduction of e-governance, various information like import-export, registration of companies, investment situations, etc. are available through the internet. As a result, time is saved, procrastination decreases and economic dynamism increases.

Reduce inequality: Using e-governance tools everyone can gather information and empower themselves. In this globalized world, knowledge is power and means of e-governance empower us by providing relevant information at minimal cost, effort and time.

Types of E Governance

E-Governance can be considered as the social inclusive policy for development of transparency and accountability of both people in society and administration. This policy involves providing the services to the people with collection of information through the institutional and communicational development.

It provides quality services in several ways. Those ways are also called as types of e-governance. These are mentioned below-

G2C (Government to Citizen)

G2G (Government to Government)

G2B (Government to Business)

G2E (Government to Employee)

1. G2C (Government to Citizen)

As people are the key concept of politics and government as well as governance, the government is compelled to connect with citizens through the transparent and accountable order. In this connection the government is responsible for promoting the social opportunities and public services in the field of

(a) Transportation (Registration of motor vehicles, Issue of driving licenses, Issue of plying permissions, Tax and fee collection through cash and bank challans and control of pollution etc.),

(b) Hospitals (linking of various hospitals in different parts of the country to ensures better medical services to citizens),

(c) Education (availability of the e-learning modules to the citizens, right to education),

(d) online job portal and various customer services.

It also ensures services such as issue of certificates, job cards, passport, ration cards, payments of bills and filing the taxes from the door step through e-governance platform. The main objectives of the G2C services are to ensure equitable distribution of information for all, acceptance of citizen's feedback and improving welfare services.

2. G2G (Government to Government)

G2G has been referring to raising the quality of the government process by cost cutting, managing performance and making strategic connections within government.

It enables government institutions to be more efficient and more effective by the use of IT tools such as-
Live fingerprints scanning and verification,
Electronic entry of reports and paperwork etc.
The major key areas in this type of e-governance are
E-Secretariat (all the valuable information regarding the function of the government are interlinking throughout the various departments),
E-Police (police personnel records, criminal records etc), and
E-Court (creating a database of all the previous cases, pending and ongoing cases) and Statewide Networks.

3. G2B (Government to Business)

G2B is mainly concerned with these things-
E-taxation,
Getting a license from the government etc.
Secure Electronics Transactions.

It has included the policy of government with business. According to S.P Kumar, 'the essentials for achievement of G2B services for secure and authentic transactions include: Standards for electronic transactions, a secure payment mechanism and Public key infrastructure'.

4. G2E (Government to Employee)

The G2E model refers to providing information and services from government to employee and employee to government as well. It involves training through-
e-learning methods;
Consolidating the employee and
Share of knowledge among the employees.

It has also facilitated the employee to access information regarding pay and benefit policies and manage their profits through online.

What is the Relation Between ICT and Governance?

Through the application of ICT in public administrations, the governing processes are more effective and more efficient and also ensure sustainable development.

ICT and Governance

Through ICT, a new forms of dialogue and collaboration among public, private and civil society organizations enhance transparency and accountability that can create conditions of fair and open while expanding access so that everyone can participate and benefit from today's knowledge-based economy.

Use of ICT in all aspects of governance can remove irrelevant human involvement in the processes of service delivery from the government to the citizens.

Hence, ICT has been promoting good governance by increasing transparency and accountability in public sectors. It helps to foster the process of decision making, public participation and reinforcing fare delivery of goods and services to the people.

In this context, the ICT developed the process of the assurance of the citizen's right to information and functions. Government sectors/institutions had been providing the information related to their accomplishments, achievements, programs and plans through their websites or e-platform to the citizens.

Citizens also can send feedback or query on any plans, programs which are mostly affected to them from their home using the ICT tools. Through the online process, people can easily upload and download forms, filing taxes, doing financial transactions through e-banking services, getting jobs through different online job portals, etc.

All the countries are interested in fostering the application of ICT in their public administrations for sustainable economic development and transparency.

World summit on Information society focused on-

An information society for all by improving access to information and communication infrastructure and technologies as well as to information and knowledge;

Capacity building

Increase confidence and security in the use of ICTs;

Create an enabling environment at all levels;

Develop and widen ICT applications; foster and respect cultural diversity; recognize the role of the media;

Address the ethical dimensions of the Information Society and encourage international and regional cooperation.

Conclusion

From the above discussion on E-Governance: Meaning, Objectives, Features and Types, it can be stated that in this era of globalization, the role of E governance is significant. This is a blessing, especially to third world countries. As a result of the implementation of e-governance, all these countries have been able to maintain their development trend on par with the developed countries. Knowledge is power. E-governance empowers ourselves by providing relevant information at minimal time, cost and price.

CHAPTER FIVE

Social Welfare Administration

Introduction

Social welfare administration is a process through which social policy is transformed into social services. It involves the administration of public and private agencies. In early times, social welfare functions were performed by a few individuals or groups of individuals motivated by compassion and concern for the poor, the needy and the destitute. These people were laymen, embodied with the qualities of humanism and selfless service to the community. But in modern times, most of the countries have adopted the concept of a welfare state instead of a police state. The Encyclopaedia of Social Sciences describes a welfare state as a state which takes up the responsibility to provide a minimum standard of subsistence to its citizens. Prof. Kent remarked that by a welfare state we mean a state which provides extensive services to the people. Thus, in a welfare state, the administration enters into economic, political, social and educational life of individuals.

And it provides services to individuals, right from an individual's birth to death. The state is to serve the old, sick, orphans, widows, helpless, oppressed and the disabled people whenever they are in need of services. Social welfare administration, it has twin concepts denoting social welfare and administration. It refers to the overall development of society having certain management from government and non-governmental guidelines. "It is the study for development", a process where providing resources and services meet the needs of individuals, groups and communities, who were poor, needy and destitute. Proper administration is needed to remove poverty, social malfunctions, child issues, women issues, etc. So for that we should work/serve for the wellbeing of the people. It is essential, where such sections of our society could get better treatment by social policymakers, planners, welfare administrators, etc. It aims to apply professional competence to achieve social work goals.

But in modern times, many of the countries have adopted the concept of a welfare state instead of a police state. The Encyclopaedia of Social Sciences describes a welfare state as a state which takes up the responsibility to provide a minimum standard of subsistence to its citizens. Prof. Kent remarked that by a welfare state we mean a state which provides extensive services to the people. Thus, in a welfare state, the administration enters into the economic, political, social and educational life of individuals. And it provides services to individuals, right from an individual's birth to death. The state is to serve the old, sick, orphans, widows, helpless, oppressed and disabled people whenever they need services. In the context of the present-day social problems, the size of welfare services provided by an increasingly large number of organizations makes administration very important. Social welfare services, schemes, projects and programmers are becoming increasingly complex. Since it is no longer accepted that any normally intelligent person with good intentions can administer the welfare work, a sound administration is vital. It is increasingly realized that social welfare programmers require qualified and trained social welfare personnel to perform social welfare functions efficiently.

Merriam Webster Dictionary defines social welfare as organized public or private social services for the assistance of disadvantaged groups.

Oxford Dictionary defines docial welfare as the well-being of society or the community at large.

Principles of social welfare administration

1. **The Principle of social work values:** Social work profession rests on values like equality, social justice and empowerment. These values also form the base upon which service delivery system of social work administration is based.
2. **The Principle of community and client needs:** The interventions carried out by the social welfare/development agencies are based on the felt needs of the community people or the target group. This is important for the acceptability of the programme.
3. **The Principle of agency purpose:** The agency should have clearly defined, formulated goals and purposes and should work in that direction only.
4. **The Principle of cultural setting:** The administrator needs to understand the socio-cultural setting of the community as it greatly influences the service acceptance and in fact success or failure of the services.
5. **The Principle of purposeful relationship:** Effective purposeful working relationship must be established between the administrator with all the stakeholders - the staff, other agencies and the community people.
6. **The Principle of agency totality:** Based on ecological approach, an agency and its functioning should be understood in its totality, which is crucial for development administration.
7. **The Principle of professional responsibility:** High professional standards of practice and accountability and responsibility should be maintained at all levels of service delivery. The principal is also linked to professional ethics of social work.
8. **The Principle of participation:** Development administration rests on people's participation in the development process right from planning to execution and evaluation of services. Democratic participation is an important aspect.
9. **The Principle of communication:** Open channels of communication are essential to effective service delivery including welfare/development interventions.
10. **The Principle of leadership:** Though democratic and participatory approaches are a must for development administration, visionary and transformational leadership is equally important for attaining the goal to overall development.
11. **The Principle of planning:** As a technical component, the process of continuous planning is fundamental to the development of meaningful services. In the context of development administration, planning has to be participatory involving the service users.
12. **The Principle of organization:** The work of many actors should be arranged in an organized manner and be structured so that responsibilities and relationships are clearly defined.
13. **The Principle of delegation:** Delegation of responsibility and authority is an important aspect in the administration process and is practiced universally in all types of administrative settings.
14. **The Principle of co-ordination:** Coordination - within the agency, with other stakeholders and outside social environment - is an important component of the administration which must be ensured for successful implementation of programs and services.
15. **The Principle of resource utilization:** Resources are almost always limited. Optimum resource utilization for maximum good is a must and it is one of the prime responsibilities of managers and administrators.
16. **The Principle of change:** Guided social change in the positive direction is the crux of social development and is crucial for social welfare/development administrators and planners.
17. **The Principle of evaluation:** Continuous evaluation of intervention processes and programs is essential to the achievement of the overall goal of holistic development.
18. **The Principle of growth:** The intervention designed should lead to holistic growth and development of all the sections of the society and should not be on ad-hoc basis or should not be confined to the betterment of a select few.

Functions of Welfare Administration

1. To formulate the appropriate objectives and programmes of the agency, it is very important to get the required information and to understand the total situation. The agency generally focuses on a particular problem in a particular geographical area.
2. To analyze the collected information so as to plan appropriate measures to solve social problems. Social welfare agency's work is to address social problems of the society in that given area.
3. To recognize, screen and opt for an appropriate plan of action to tackle problems and handle the initiatives of the social welfare agency.
4. Formulating policies, programmes and plans for effectively carrying out the objectives of the social welfare agency in a planned manner.
5. To identify appropriate personnel for the social welfare agency with proper orientation and supervision so that they understand the objectives and how to implement the programs in order to achieve the goals of the agency.
6. To inspire volunteers who can involve themselves in the aims, objectives and goals of the social welfare agency.
7. The administration has to delegate work to various departments under supervisors who will be accountable for the assigned work in the various departments which has to be coordinated so that maximum results are obtained.
8. Rules, regulations, practices and procedures have to be set up so that there is uniformity and accountability among all staff in the agency so that the objectives of the agency are easily accomplished.
9. The agency must keep proper records and reports. These records and reports must be analyzed and interpreted to find out the progress of the agency's work.
10. The financial practices must be very economically and strictly laid down so that there can be no misappropriations. The finances must be accurately utilized and accounted for finance is the backbone of any organization. So finances must be properly managed.
11. Every agency has to lay down certain standards of work and work towards meeting those standards at all times. The personnel from highest level to the lowest level must understand and maintain the standards and work for it with great care.

Features of social welfare administration

Although the concept of administration is applicable in a broader sense to areas including social welfare, business and government, there are certain distinctive features of social welfare administration. A summary of features highlighting the distinctiveness of social welfare administration is given below:

1. It is concerned with social agencies and helps them to achieve their objectives within the target community. It is specifically concerned with the identification of social objectives and formulation/implementation of programs.
2. From a functional point of view, it encompasses three facets of social problems: (i) Restoration of impaired social functioning; (ii) Provision of resources, social and individual for more effective social functioning; (iii) Prevention of social dysfunction.
3. Despite variations in size, scope, structure and type of programs, every agency has a governing board as an apex body for final decision making. The board is generally represented by the community it intends to serve.
4. Social welfare administration requires optimum utilization of its available resources together with active community participation so that the ultimate goal of programs can be achieved properly.
5. Social welfare agencies have to earmark a certain portion of their resources for survival. But this should not limit their capacity to achieve in quantitative and qualitative terms.
6. Social welfare agencies generally function in a cooperative manner and ensure participation of all the members in the administration of their activities.
7. There is a growing trend in these agencies to recruit professionally qualified manpower. It has helped in introducing a professional approach in their functioning.

Functions of Welfare Administration

- To formulate the appropriate objectives and programmes of the agency, it is very important to get the required information and to understand the total situation. The agency generally focuses on a particular problem in a particular geographical area.
- To analyze the collected information so as to plan appropriate measures to solve social problems. Social welfare agency's work is to address social problems of the society in that given area.
- To recognize, screen and opt for an appropriate plan of action to tackle problems and handle the initiatives of the social welfare agency.
- Formulating policies, programmes and plans for effectively carrying out the objectives of the social welfare agency in a planned manner.
- To identify appropriate personnel for the social welfare agency with proper orientation and supervision so that they understand the objectives and how to implement the programmes in order to achieve the goals of the agency.
- To inspire volunteers who can involve themselves in the aims, objectives and goals of the social welfare agency.
- The administration has to delegate work to various departments under supervisors who will be accountable for the assigned work in the various departments which has to be coordinated so that maximum results are obtained.
- Rules, regulations, practices and procedures have to be set up so that there is uniformity and accountability among all staff in the agency so that the objectives of the agency are easily accomplished.
- The agency must keep proper records and reports. These records and reports must be analyzed and interpreted to find out the progress of the agency's work.
- The financial practices must be very economically and strictly laid down so that there can be no misappropriations. The finances must be accurately utilized and accounted for finance is the backbone of any organization. So finances must be properly managed.
- Every agency has to lay down certain standards of work and work towards meeting those standards at all times. The personnel from the highest level to the lowest level must understand and maintain the standards and work for it with great care.
- One of the main threads that binds the whole agency together is communication. The communication must be clear and smooth from all sectors of the agency be it horizontal from department to department or vertical from top to bottom or bottom to top. The agency must also have an open communication channel with the community people.
- Social welfare administration must also see to it that the agency has suitable coordination within the various departments of the agency and at various levels in the agency. The agency when it works as a whole, it becomes most effective to meet its objectives. The social welfare agency must also have proper coordination with other agencies working in the same field. There must be networking with agencies with similar themes in some geographical areas.

Scope of Social Welfare Administration

Social welfare administration is basically the execution of social policies, social programs and social legislations by philanthropic, religious and charitable organizations, which provide services and benefits for the general population in need. It is the conversion of social policy into social action and how welfare state virtues are translated into action and implemented by social welfare agencies. A very comprehensive understanding on the scope of social welfare administration that has been put forth by Titmus (1958) is: "Social welfare administration may be defined as the study of social services whose object is the improvement of conditions of life of the individual in the settling of family and group relations."

The POSDCORB view: This view of social welfare administration takes into account mostly the execution of the government's sponsored programs. In other words, this view corresponds with a managerial view. Henri Fayol, L.

Urwick, Fercey M. Ovean and Luther Gulick are advocates of this view. According to Henri Fayol, the main categories of administration are:

There are broadly two views about the scope of social welfare administration. These are

(i) The POSDCORB view: This view of social welfare administration takes into account mostly the execution of the government's sponsored programs. In other words, this view corresponds with a managerial view. Henri Fayol, L. Urwick, Fercey M. Ocean and Luther Gulick are advocates of this view. According to Henri Fayol the main categories of administration are:

1. Organization
2. Coordination and
3. Control Command

P.M. Queen says that the study of administration deals with the three 'm' that is 'men, material and methods'. L. Gulick has given a magic formula in a word 'POSDCORB' that is very popular. In POSDCORB each a letter describing one technique. These letters stand for:

1. P Planning
2. O Organising
3. S Staffing
4. D Directing
5. Co Coordinating
6. R Reporting
7. B Budgeting

In the recent years both academics and practitioners in India have added two more meaningful words to complete the techniques namely: E Evaluation and F Feedback.

Areas of Social welfare administration

1. Organization and structure
2. Public relations
3. Maintenance of proper record
4. Policymaking and planning
5. Supervision and leadership

Conclusion

A social worker to be a professional is incomplete without the Social Welfare Administration. Social Worker aims to provide service to every individual in the society and social welfare administration is not a business of social work. The welfare administration helps professionally doing social work in society. It is a secondary method that helps social workers to solve their facing problems. It offers an opportunity for social workers to practice in the field. Without any administration, we cannot get a solution through practice.

In modern times, all human activities are concerned with money. But in a profession, an effort is made to see that service motto should prevail over monetary considerations. Professionals should keep social interest in their minds while charging fees for their professional services. For example, a doctor helps the patient, not only to charge a fee, but also to serve humanity in the process. A lawyer helps the client, not to charge the fee only, but to provide justice to the client. Similarly, a social welfare administrator administers the social welfare programmers, not only for money and personal satisfaction, but uses his/her knowledge and skills to serve the larger interest of the society.

Right to Education

The Right of Children to Free and Compulsory Education Act or Right to Education Act (RTE) is an Act of the Parliament of India enacted on 4 August 2009, which describes the modalities of the importance of free and compulsory education for children between 6 and 14 in India under Article 21a of the Indian Constitution. India became one of 135 countries to make education a fundamental right of every child when the Act came into force on 1 April 2010.

The Act makes education a fundamental right of every child between the ages of 6 and 14 and specifies minimum norms in elementary schools. It requires all private schools to reserve 25% of seats to children (to be reimbursed by the state as part of the public-private partnership plan). Kids are admitted in to private schools based on economic status or caste based reservations. It also prohibits all unrecognised schools from practice and makes provisions for no donation or capitation fees and no interview of the child or parent for admission. The Act also provides that no child shall be held back, expelled or required to pass a board examination until the completion of elementary education. There is also a provision for special training of school drop-outs to bring them up to par with students of the same age.

The RTE Act requires surveys that will monitor all neighbourhoods, identify children requiring education and set up facilities for providing it. The World Bank education specialist for India, Sam Carlson has observed: "The RTE Act is the first legislation in the world that puts the responsibility of ensuring enrolment, attendance and completion on the Government. It is the parents' responsibility to send the children to schools in the US and other countries."

The Right to Education of persons with disabilities until 18 years of age is laid down under a separate legislation - the Persons with Disabilities Act. A number of other provisions regarding improvement of school infrastructure, teacher-student ratio and faculty are made in the Act.

Education in the Indian constitution is a concurrent issue and both centre and states can legislate on the issue. The Act lays down specific responsibilities for the centre, state and local bodies for its implementation. The states have been clamouring that they lack financial capacity to deliver education of appropriate standard in all the schools needed for universal education. Thus it was clear that the central government (which collects most of the revenue) will be required to subsidise the states.

A committee set up to study the funds requirement and funding initially estimated that INR 1710 billion or 1.71 trillion (US$38.2 billion) across five years was required to implement the Act and in April 2010 the central government agreed to sharing the funding for implementing the law in the ratio of 65 to 35 between the centre and the states and a ratio of 90 to 10 for the north-eastern states. However, in mid 2010, this figure was upgraded to INR 2310 billion and the center agreed to raise its share to 68%. There is some confusion on this, with other media reports stating that the centre's share of the implementation expenses would now be 70%. At that rate, most states may not need to increase their education budgets substantially.

A critical development in 2011 has been the decision taken in principle to extend the right to education till Class X (age 16) and into the preschool age range. The CABE committee is in the process of looking into the implications of making these changes.

The Ministry of HRD set up a high-level 14-member National Advisory Council (NAC) for implementation of the Act. The members included Kiran Karnik, former president of NASSCOM; Krishna Kumar, former director of the NCERT; Mrinal Miri, former vice-chancellor of North-East Hill University; Yogendra Yadav – social scientist; Sajit Krishnan Kutty, Secretary of The Educators Assisting Children's Hopes (TEACH) India; Annie Namala, an activist and head of Centre for Social Equity and Inclusion; and Aboobacker Ahmad, vice-president of Muslim Education Society, Kerala.

A report on the status of implementation of the Act was released by the Ministry of Human Resource Development on the one year anniversary of the Act. The report admits that 8.1 million children in the age group 6-14 remain out of school and there's a shortage of 508,000 teachers country-wide. A shadow report by the RTE Forum representing the leading education networks in the country, however, challenging the findings pointing out that several key legal commitments are falling behind the schedule. The Supreme Court of India has also intervened to demand implementation of the Act in the Northeast. It has also provided the legal basis for ensuring pay parity between teachers in government and government aided schools. Haryana Government has assigned the duties and responsibilities to Block Elementary Education Officers–cum–Block Resource Coordinators (BEEOs-cum-BRCs) for effective implementation and continuous monitoring of implementation of Right to Education Act in the State.

It has been pointed out that the RTE act is not new. Universal adult franchise in the act was opposed since most of the population was illiterate. Article 45 in the Constitution of India was set up as an act: The State shall endeavour to provide, within a period of ten years from the commencement of this Constitution, for free and compulsory education for all children until they complete the age of fourteen years.

As that deadline was about to be passed many decades ago, the education minister at the time, MC Chagla, memorably said: "Our Constitution fathers did not intend that we just set up hovels, put students there, give untrained teachers, give them bad textbooks, no playgrounds, and say, we have complied with Article 45 and primary education is expanding... They meant that real education should be given to our children between the ages of 6 and 14" - (MC Chagla, 1964).

In the 1990s, the World Bank funded a number of measures to set up schools within easy reach of rural communities. This effort was consolidated in the Sarva Shiksha Abhiyan model in the 1990s. RTE takes the process further and makes the enrolment of children in schools a state prerogative.

National Health Mission

Recently, the Union Minister of State for Health and Family Welfare informed the Rajya Sabha that National Health Mission (NHM) supported health system reforms have resulted in development of resilient health systems.

NHM was launched by the government of India in 2013 subsuming the National Rural Health Mission (Launched in 2005) and the National Urban Health Mission (Launched in 2013).

The main programmatic components include Health System Strengthening in rural and urban areas for Reproductive-Maternal-Neonatal-Child and Adolescent Health (RMNCH+A) and Communicable and Non-Communicable Diseases.

The NHM envisages achievement of universal access to equitable, affordable & quality health care services that are accountable and responsive to people's needs.

Support to States & Union Territories (UT):

Health Facilities:

NHM support is provided to States/UTs for setting up of new facilities as per norms and upgradation of existing facilities for bridging the infrastructure gaps based on the requirement posed by them.

Health Services:

NHM support is also provided for provision of a range of free services related to maternal health, child health, adolescent health, family planning, universal immunisation programme and for major diseases such as Tuberculosis, vector borne diseases like Malaria, Dengue and Kala Azar, Leprosy, etc.

Major Initiatives Supported Under NHM:

Janani Shishu Suraksha Karyakram (JSSK).

Rashtriya Bal Swasthya Karyakram (RBSK).

Implementation of Free Drugs and Free Diagnostics Service Initiatives.

PM National Dialysis Programme.

Implementation of National Quality Assurance Framework in all public health facilities.

Mobile Medical Units (MMUs) & Tele-consultation services are also being implemented to improve access to healthcare particularly in rural areas.

Ayushman Bharat.

Pradhan Mantri Jan Arogya Yojana (AB-PMJAY).

Achievements of NHM

Improvement in Health Indicators:

In the 15 years of implementation, the NHM has enabled achievement of the Millennium Development Goals (MDGs) for health.

The MDGs have been superseded by the Sustainable Development Goals.

It has also led to significant improvements in maternal, new-born and child health indicators, particularly for maternal mortality ratio, infant and under five mortality rates, wherein the rates of decline in India are much higher than the global averages and these declines have accelerated during the period of implementation of NHM.

Growth in Public Health Facilities:

NHM adopts a health system approach and targets to build a network for public health facilities with Health & Wellness Centres at the grassroot level and District Hospitals with robust referral linkage to offer Comprehensive primary and secondary care services to citizens.

NHM has not only contributed to increase in the institutional capacities for service delivery but also has led to development of capacities for targeted interventions of the various National Programmes under the NHM.

Equitable Development:

There was also a sustained focus on the health of tribal populations, those in Left Wing Extremism areas and the urban poor.

A more recent effort at ensuring equity in access and use is the Aspirational district initiative in which 115 districts across 28 states with weak social and human development indicators have been identified for allocation of additional resources and capacity enhancement to catch up with more progressive districts.

National Ambulance Services:

At the time of launch of NRHM (2005), ambulance networks were non-existent.

So far 20,990 Emergency Response Service Vehicles are operational under NRHM.

Besides 5,499 patient transport vehicles are also deployed, particularly for providing "free pickup and drop back" facilities to pregnant women and sick infants.

Human Resource Augmentation:

NHM supports states for engaging service delivery HR such as doctors, nurses and health workers and also implements the world's largest community health volunteer programme through the Accredited Social Health Activists (ASHAs).

More than 10 lakhs ASHAs and ASHA facilitators are engaged under NHM.

NHM has also supported states to acquire staff with skills in public health, finance, planning and management to plan and implement interventions, freeing up clinical staff to deliver health services.

Health Sector Reforms:

NHM enabled the design and implementation of reforms specifically related to Governance, Procurement and Technology.

Addressing high Out-of-Pocket Expenditure (OOPE):

Recognising the need for reducing the current high levels of OOPE and that, almost 70% of the OOPE is on account of drugs and diagnostics, the Free Drugs and Free Diagnostics Services Initiatives have been implemented under the NHM.

The National List of Essential Medicines (NLEM) and the Essential Diagnostics Lists have been notified and are periodically updated to include more essential drugs based on new initiatives undertaken.

Right to Food Security

As per the Economic Survey (2018-19), India needs to take big initiatives to improve its food security as it faces supply constraints, water scarcity, small landholdings, low per capita GDP and inadequate irrigation.

What is Food Security?

Food security, as defined by the United Nations' Committee on World Food Security, means that all people, at all times, have physical, social and economic access to sufficient, safe and nutritious food that meets their food preferences and dietary needs for an active and healthy life.

Food security is the combination of the following three elements:

Food availability i.e. food must be available in sufficient quantities and on a consistent basis. It considers stock and production in a given area and the capacity to bring in food from elsewhere, through trade or aid.

Food access i.e. people must be able to regularly acquire adequate quantities of food, through purchase, home production, barter, gifts, borrowing or food aid.

Food utilization: Consumed food must have a positive nutritional impact on people. It entails cooking, storage and hygiene practices, individuals health, water and sanitations, feeding and sharing practices within the household.

Food security is closely related to household resources, disposable income and socioeconomic status. It is also strongly interlinked with other issues such as food prices, global environment change, water, energy and agriculture growth.

Why Food Security is Important for a Nation?

For boosting the agricultural sector.

For having a control on food prices.

For economic growth and job creation leading to poverty reduction.

For trade opportunities.

For increased global security and stability.

For improved health and healthcare.

Food Security in India

Food security concerns can be traced back to the experience of the Bengal Famine in 1943 during British colonial rule during which about 2 million to 3 million people perished due to starvation.

Since attaining independence, an initial rush to industrialize while ignoring agriculture, two successive droughts in the mid-1960s and dependence on food aid from the United States exposed India's vulnerability to several shocks on the food security front.

The country went through a Green Revolution in the late 1960s and early 1970s enabling it to overcome productivity stagnation and to significantly improve food grain production.

Despite its success, the Green Revolution is often criticized for being focused on only two cereals: wheat and rice being confined to a few resource abundant regions in the northwestern and southern parts of the country that benefited mostly rich farmers and putting too much stress on the ecology of these regions, especially soil and water.

The Green Revolution was followed by the White Revolution, which was initiated by Operation Flood during the 1970s and 1980s. This national initiative has revolutionized liquid milk production and marketing in India, making it the largest producer of milk.

Of late, especially during the post-2000 period, hybrid maize for poultry and industrial use and Bacillus thuringiensis (Bt) cotton have shown great strides in production, leading to sizeable exports of cotton, which made India the second largest exporter of cotton in 2007–2008.

Concerns vis-a-vis Food Security in India

India, currently has the largest number of undernourished people in the world i.e. around 195 million.

Nearly 47 million or 4 out of 10 children in India do not meet their full human potential because of chronic undernutrition or stunting.

Agricultural productivity in India is extremely low.

According to World Bank figures, cereal yield in India is estimated to be 2,992 kg per hectare as against 7,318.4 kg per hectare in North America.

The composition of the food basket is increasingly shifting away from cereals to high—value agricultural commodities like fish, eggs, milk and meat. As incomes continue to rise, this trend will continue and the indirect demand for food from feed will grow rapidly in India.

According to FAO estimates in 'The State of Food Security and Nutrition in the World, 2018" report, about 14.8% of the population is undernourished in India.

Also, 51.4% of women in reproductive age between 15 to 49 years are anaemic.

Further according to the report 38.4% of children aged under five in India are stunted (too short for their age), while 21% suffer from wasting, meaning their weight is too low for their height.

India ranked 76th in 113 countries assessed by The Global Food Security Index (GFSI) in the year 2018, based on four parameters—affordability, availability and quality and safety.

As per the Global Hunger Index, 2018, India was ranked 103rd out of 119 qualifying countries.

Challenges to Food Security

Climate Change: Higher temperatures and unreliable rainfall makes farming difficult. Climate change not only impacts crop, but also livestock, forestry, fisheries and aquaculture and can cause grave social and economic consequences in the form of reduced incomes, eroded livelihoods, trade disruption and adverse health impacts.

Lack of access to remote areas: For the tribal communities, habitation in remote difficult terrains and practice of subsistence farming has led to significant economic backwardness.

Increase in rural-to-urban migration, large proportion of informal workforce resulting in unplanned growth of slums which lack in the basic health and hygiene facilities, insufficient housing and increased food insecurity.

Overpopulation, poverty, lack of education and gender inequality: Inadequate distribution of food through public distribution mechanisms (PDS i.e. Public Distribution System).

Deserving beneficiaries of the subsidy are excluded on the basis of non-ownership of below poverty line (BPL) status as the criterion for identifying a household as BPL is arbitrary and varies from state to state.

Biofuels: The growth of the biofuel market has reduced the land used for growing food crops.

Conflict: Food can be used as a weapon with enemies cutting off food supplies in order to gain ground. Crops can also be destroyed during the conflict.

Unmonitored nutrition programmes: Although a number of programmes with improving nutrition as their main component are planned in the country but these are not properly implemented.

Lack of coherent food and nutrition policies along with the absence of intersectoral coordination between various ministries.

Corruption: Diverting the grains to open market to get better margin, selling poor quality grains at ration shops and irregular opening of the shops add to the issue of food insecurity.

Recent Government Initiatives

National Food Security Mission

It is a Centrally Sponsored Scheme launched in 2007.

It aims to increase production of rice, wheat, pulses, coarse cereals and commercial crops through area expansion and productivity enhancement.

It works toward restoring soil fertility and productivity at the individual farm level and enhancing farm level economy.

It further aims to augment the availability of vegetable oils and to reduce the import of edible oils.

Rashtriya Krishi Vikas Yojana (RKVY)

It was initiated in 2007 and allowed states to choose their own agriculture and allied sector development activities as per the district/state agriculture plan.

It was converted into a Centrally Sponsored Scheme in 2014-15 also with 100% central assistance.

Rashtriya Krishi Vikas Yojana (RKVY) has been named as Rashtriya Krishi Vikas Yojana - Remunerative Approaches for Agriculture and Allied Sector Rejuvenation (RKVY-RAFTAAR) for three years i.e. from 2017-18 to 2019-20.

Objectives: Making farming a remunerative economic activity through strengthening the farmer's effort, risk mitigation and promoting agri-business entrepreneurship. Major focus is on pre & post-harvest infrastructure, besides promoting agri-entrepreneurship and innovations.

Integrated Schemes on Oilseeds, Pulses, Palm oil and Maize (ISOPOM)

Pradhan Mantri Fasal Bima Yojana

E-marketplace: The government has created an electronic national agriculture market (eNAM) to connect all regulated wholesale produce markets through a pan-India trading portal.

Massive irrigation and soil and water harvesting programme to increase the country's gross irrigated area from 90 million hectares to 103 million hectares by 2017.

The government has also taken significant steps to combat under and malnutrition over the past two decades, through the introduction of mid-day meals at schools. It is a Centrally-Sponsored Scheme which covers all school children studying in Classes I-VIII of Government and Government-Aided Schools.

Anganwadi systems to provide rations to pregnant and lactating mothers.

Subsidised grain for those living below the poverty line through a public distribution system.

Food fortification

The National Food Security Act (NFSA), 2013, legally entitles up to 75% of the rural population and 50% of the urban population to receive subsidized food grains under the Targeted Public Distribution System.

The eldest woman of the household of age 18 years or above is mandated to be the head of the household for the purpose of issuing of ration cards under the Act.

International Organizations involved in ensuring Food Security

Food and Agricultural Organization (FAO)

Established as a specialized agency of the United Nations in 1945.

One of FAO's strategic objectives is to help eliminate hunger, food insecurity and malnutrition.

World Food Programme (WFP)

Founded in 1963, WFP is the lead UN agency that responds to food emergencies and has programmes to combat hunger worldwide.

International Fund for Agricultural Development (IFAD)

Founded in 1977, IFAD focuses on rural poverty reduction, working with poor rural populations in developing countries to eliminate poverty, hunger and malnutrition.

It is a specialized agency of the United Nations and was one of the major outcomes of the 1974 World Food Conference.

World Bank

Founded in 1944, the World Bank is actively involved in funding food projects and programmes.

United Nations Environment Programme (UNEP)

It was established in 1972 as the international arm providing guidance and governance to environmental issues. One of the topics that UNEP addresses currently is food security.

International Initiatives

The High-Level Task Force (HLTF) on Global Food and Nutrition Security was established by the UN Secretary-General Ban Ki-moon in 2008.

It aims to promote a comprehensive and unified response of the international community to the challenge of achieving global food and nutrition security.

Formulation of the First Millennium Development Goal (MDG 1), which included among its targets cutting by half the proportion of people who suffer from hunger by 2015.

The United Nations Secretary-General launched the Zero Hunger Challenge in 2012 during the Rio+20 World Conference on Sustainable Development. The Zero Hunger Challenge was launched to inspire a global movement towards a world free from hunger within a generation. It calls for:

Zero stunted children under the age of two

100% access to adequate food all year round

All food systems are sustainable

100% increase in smallholder productivity and income

Zero loss or waste of food

SDG Goal 2 - End hunger, achieve food security and improved nutrition and promote sustainable agriculture.

Steps to be Taken to Ensure Food Security

The government policy needs to adopt an integrated policy framework to facilitate agriculture productivity.

The measures should focus mainly on rationale distribution of cultivable land, improving the size of the farms and providing security to the tenant cultivators apart from providing the farmers with improved technology for cultivation and improved inputs like irrigation facilities, availability of better quality seeds, fertilizers and credits at lower interest rates.

Aeroponics and hydroponics are systems that allow plants to be grown without soil. Plants grown in this way take in water and nutrients efficiently. These methods can be used in the areas of poor soil quality and soil erosion.

Adoption of crops and techniques with lower water requirements, such as the System of Rice Intensification (SRI) method of rice production, contributes to resilience by enabling equal or better yields to be achieved with less water withdrawal.

Planting crops with lower water requirements and agricultural practices that maintain soil moisture, such as maintaining vegetative cover between crops, can also contribute to resilience.

Crop diversification: Higher profitability and stability in production highlight the importance of crop diversification, e.g. legumes alternative with rice and wheat. Growing of non-cereal crops such as oilseeds, fruits and vegetables, etc. need to be encouraged.

Strategies for better food storage should be adopted.

The Blue Revolution: Sea, lakes and rivers can be used to provide food and nutrition. Fish are a very good source of protein and do not require good soil.

Biotechnology and appropriate technology: Selective breeding or genetic modification (GM) of plants and animals can be done to produce specific features and adaptations.

For example, selective breeding has been used on dairy cows to increase milk yields. GM has been used on wheat to produce crops that are disease resistant.

Existing direct nutrition programmes should be revamped to enable management by women's Self Help Groups (SHGs) and/or local bodies along with orientation and training of community health workers, Panchayati Raj Institution (PRI) members, other opinion leaders, caregivers and other stakeholders can be another area.

Efforts should be made by the concerned health departments and authorities to initiate and supervise the functioning of the nutrition related schemes in an efficient way.

Annual surveys and rapid assessments surveys could be some of the ways through which program outcomes can be measured.

Focus needs to be shifted to the workers in the informal sector by providing decent wages and healthy working conditions.

Local community education on key family health and nutrition practices using participatory and planned communication methodologies will be helpful.

The cooperatives play an important role in food security in India especially in the southern and western parts of the country. The cooperative societies set up shops to sell low priced goods to poor people. The cooperatives should be encouraged.

Fostering rural-urban economic linkages can be an important step towards ensuring food security by

enhancing and diversifying rural employment opportunities especially for women and youth,

enabling the poor to better manage risks through social protection and leveraging remittances for investments in the rural sector as a viable means for improving livelihoods.

Way Forward

Food security of a nation is ensured if all of its citizens have enough nutritious food available, all persons have the capacity to buy food of acceptable quality and there is no barrier on access to food.

The right to food is a well established principle of international human rights law. It has evolved to include an obligation for state parties to respect, protect and fulfil their citizens' right to food security.

As a state party to the Universal Declaration of Human Rights and the International Covenant on Economic, Social and Cultural Rights, India has the obligation to ensure the right to be free from hunger and the right to adequate food.

India needs to adopt a policy that brings together diverse issues such as inequality, food diversity, indigenous rights and environmental justice to ensure sustainable food security.

The Mahatma Gandhi National Rural Employment Guarantee Act

The Mahatma Gandhi National Rural Employment Guarantee Act (MNREGA) was adopted in 2005 and first became operational in 200 of the poorest districts in India in February 2006. Within two and a half years it was extended to the rest of the country in April 2008.

This Act was a ground-breaking; although there had been similar employment generating programmes before, it was the first time the right to work had been legally recognised. Development in recent years in India has been spearheaded by a rights-based approach and a legal guarantee of entitlements. In 2009 the Right to Education Act was passed that bestowed the right to free and compulsory education to children between the ages of 6 and 14. There are currently talks about implementing the Right to Food as a corollary of the Right to Life (Article 21 of the Constitution) to prevent hunger and starvation in the country.

In India, over 70% of the population lives in villages and the rural economy depends heavily on agriculture. Consequently, there is a major problem of seasonal employment and large numbers among the rural population migrate in search of work to other regions during the slack season.

The MNREGA plays a significant role in this regard by providing a legal guarantee of 100 days of employment in every financial year to adult members of all rural households willing to do public work-related unskilled manual work at a minimum wage. According to the provisions of the Act, work needs to be provided to a person who registers for it within fifteen days of the date of demand, failing which they are eligible to receive an unemployment allowance from the state government. Therefore, the Act acts as a social safety net, provides employment to the poorest and aims at inclusive growth and strengthening of the rural economy.

Inclusive growth

MNREGA has succeeded in increasing employment better than any previous government scheme. However, the success of MNREGA needs to me measured on various other parameters; apart from generating employment it also aims to achieve other socio-economic goals. For one, being intrinsically self targeting, it promotes the social inclusion and economic empowerment of marginalised groups. According to the National Report 2010-2011 by the Ministry of Rural Development that oversees the implementation of the scheme, the Scheduled Castes comprise 22.56% of person-days and the Scheduled Tribes comprise 17.27% of person-days. Considering the rural setup where the caste system continues to dominate the social order and deny the backward communities their rights, this is significant and could play a role in improving the condition and be an entry point for their involvement in local self government.

Further, MNREGA has also sought to involve women to a large extent. It not only provides them with the opportunity to be engaged in gainful employment, but also promotes gender equality by setting an equal wage rate for males and females. While the Act is committed to ensuring that at least 33% of the workers are women, these expectations have been surpassed in most states. The National Report 2010-2011 attributes 51.11% of person-days to women. It is therefore aiding in promoting the economic freedom and empowerment of women in rural areas through their financial independence.

The implementation of MNREGA could through the macroeconomic concepts of the multiplier and accelerator stimulate further growth in rural India. MNREGA being self targeting creates purchasing power among the economically weak sections. Their demand for commodities results in investment for increased production, which in turn generates additional income. This process (the multiplier effect) depends on the marginal propensity to consume (MPC) of those affected. Seeing as those benefiting are at the bottom of the pyramid, their MPC is high and therefore the effect of the multiplier is strong.

Rural infrastructure and employment

Another key focus of the Act is to create durable assets in rural areas and thereby advance the rural economy and encourage sustainable development. Projects related to rural connectivity, irrigation, flood control and drought proofing, land development are taken up to raise agricultural productivity.

Apart from this, job creation in rural areas is meant to prevent migration. There are reports that the participation of women is high because they find is a good source of additional income while being able to stay in their own village, while the men migrate to other areas for work. It was also aimed at preventing seasonal migration during the slack season of agriculture with the hope that it will prevent disruption of the education of rural children. However, the guarantee of one 100 days of work a year is often left unfulfilled and therefore MNREGA has not been completely successful in curbing distress migration.

On the other hand, the World Bank in its World Development Report 2009 criticised MNREGA due to its negative impact on economic growth by discouraging rural-urban migration. According to the report development requires urbanisation and the government should not fight the tendency of economic activity being concentrated in a few regions. However, the massive population of India and the existing high population density in the large cities makes it very difficult for the physical and social infrastructure to accommodate the volume of migrants that come in. Consequently, although labourers may receive higher wages than in the villages, they often have to endure terrible living and working conditions in the cities.

With this in mind, although urban centres are important for development, without adequate infrastructure rural-urban migration in large numbers proves to be a burden and therefore the creation of jobs in rural areas is required.

In such a case, creation of infrastructure such as roads and electricity can create jobs in rural areas and aid the transformation of villages into towns. The state of Tamil Nadu, which has been very effective in implementing MNREGA is the most urbanised state in the country and has succeeded in this objective by focusing on the development of smaller towns rather than larger cities.

Impact on wages

An expected spill over of the scheme has been a significant rise in market wages in rural areas in almost all states. However, critics have held the scheme responsible for the shortages seen in the supply of agricultural labour which has resulted in agriculture becoming unviable and food prices increasing. On the one hand, agricultural labourers deserve a fair wage and in this regard MNREGA has paid a positive role.

On the other hand, in light of the problems faced by the agricultural sector, some consider this increase in wages a distortion in the labour market that is leading to inefficiencies and increased costs. The labour shortage is forcing farmers to incur added costs to replace the cheap migrant labourers with machines. The increased prices of agricultural goods have a negative impact and affect those living on the margins the most as they are most vulnerable to price increases. Therefore, some farmer's groups have suggested that the 100 days work be provided only during the lean season for agriculture but this has not been implemented yet.

Corruption and delays

A common complaint is that of delays at every stage - a person who registers for employment is supposed to be provided with a job within 15 days failing which he/she should be able to claim an unemployment allowance. Further, the Act makes provisions requiring wages to be paid within 15 days of employment. However, there are constant delays in payments and workers often wait for months to receive their wages. Delayed wages warrant compensation under the Payment of Wages Act. However, due to an ineffective grievance mechanism the problem has not been addressed.

Further, the national average for 2008-2009 was 48 days of employment per household as opposed to the guarantee of 100 days. No state has effectively implemented the unemployment benefit mechanism and those that are not being given their 100 days of work are not being paid any allowance.

Another problem faced in execution is that of corruption and leakages of funds. Although the Act emphasises transparency, some areas still witness high levels of corruption. For instance, public works in Orissa still follow the PC system where contractors, engineers and other officials demand a fixed percentage of the outlay. Jean Dreze, a development economist and one of the architects of the MNREGA, told us on December 17, 2010 at a talk at St Xavier's College that in areas where the PC system is in place intermediaries taking a cut out of the funds is not even considered corruption provided they take their regular percentage cut-only any amount beyond that was regarded as corrupt practice.

Still, since the implementation of MNREGA, corruption has started coming down. Social audits are conducted to monitor the working of the scheme, many of the muster rolls are available online and the people are gradually becoming more aware and are therefore able to monitor the system and ensure payment. The Act mentions a variety of transparency safeguards. Attempts must be made to enforce them and punish those that indulge in corrupt practices.

In an attempt to reduce corruption the wages are to be paid through bank accounts and post office deposits to ensure that the entire amount goes to the labourers. However, the sudden shift caused problems of its own. The banking system is finding it difficult to handle the volume of transactions which is leading to delays in wage payments. It is also creating hardship for the labourers that live in remote areas and have to travel long distances to access banks. Nevertheless it is a move in the positive direction and will play a role in improving the penetration of the banking system in rural India.

Another move to reduce corruption under the contractor system which involved contractors siphoning a percentage of the total project costs was the requirement under the Act that 60% of the total outlay for a project needs to go to the labourers. However, a downside of this constraint is that it often results in the creation of assets that do not last for long, such as temporary mud roads and therefore do not aid in rural development effectively.

Implementation problems

One of the major hurdles is the lack of cooperation between the state governments and the centre. Enthusiasm among the states has been inconsistent and the poorest states of Bihar, Orissa and Jharkhand have not implemented it effectively. State governments have employment guarantee schemes and need to co-ordinate with the central government. The absence of such a co-operation adversely affects the functioning of the scheme.

Another problem is the lack of suitable staff, a people-centred programme such as the NREGS requires a dedicated human resource staff. However, there is too much bureaucratic control. Further, there is a shortage of technical staff such as engineers leading to the construction of inefficient projects.

Conclusion

The Mahatma Gandhi National Rural Employment Guarantee Act was the first attempt to codify development rights in a legal context. Although it is not the key to the rejuvenation of rural areas or the end of poverty in India, it is a chance for the rural poor that live on the margins to stake a small claim in the development process. India has over 260 million people living below poverty line. MNREGA - although not flawless, could prove to be their chance to rise out of absolute poverty and begin to reap the fruits of development the rest of the country is enjoying.

Approaches of Social Welfare

1. Correctional approach- When the goals are set up for a social policy, then it is necessary to determine the means to achieve it. Rearrangements are essential for the welfare of the society but when the rearrangements are not possible then desired changes are made. These desired changes are social reforms. Through these desired changes goals of social welfare are achieved. The system of law plays an important role in the progressive process of the reforms. Social reforms have been getting legitimacy through social laws.

2. Protection approach- Damage, accident, sickness, inability and unemployment are the conditions in a person's life when external help becomes necessary for them. Therefore the system of protection against these different types of risk is called social security. It is an important foundation for the attainment of social welfare. Under this social insurance, social assistance and business insurance schemes are included.

3. Democratic approach- Initially the social welfare was limited to the individual, family, business associations and religious people. Until the nineteenth century it was believed that no state intervention was required for social welfare. According to the development theory the person who does not have ability to live, nature ends itself. But this attitude changed.

4. Community approach: The state and the individuals are equally responsible for the welfare, therefore under the five year plans in India, community approach has been adopted to fulfill the goal of welfare works. An attempt is made to develop social welfare work to an extent where the local community is ready to bear the responsibility of these welfare works. While conducting the scheme, care has been taken to ensure that it is beneficial for all the parts of society.